AN AUCTIONEER'S LOT

Tales of a country auctioneer...

From priceless eighteenth-century tables hidden away in decaying farm sheds to tattooed travellers with a penchant for Worcester china, professional auctioneer Philip Serrell has seen it all. For over twenty years he has uncovered a huge range of priceless (and occasionally worthless) antiques, and he has met, done business with and befriended people from some odd corners of English life. Funny, startling and sometimes poignant, these stories of ordinary people with extraordinary possessions are also the perfect inspiration for anyone who's ever wondered whether they might just be sitting on a fortune...

AN AUCTIONEER'S LOT

An Auctioneer's Lot

by

Philip Serrell

Magna Large Print Books
Long Preston, North Yorkshire,
BD23 4ND, England.

British Library Cataloguing in Publication Data.

Serrell, Philip
  An auctioneer's lot.

  A catalogue record of this book is
  available from the British Library

  ISBN 0-7505-2509-6

First published in Great Britain 2005 by Hodder & Stoughton
A division of Hodder Headline

Magna Large Print is an imprint of Library Magna Books Ltd.

Printed and bound in Great Britain by
T.J. (International) Ltd., Cornwall, PL28 8RW

"TED".

with thanks to B. & C.S.; J., M. & W.R.; E.B.; L.B.; D.S.; R.T.; R.L.; et al.

Contents

Author's Note

I have thoroughly enjoyed my time as an auctioneer and valuer, travelling around rural Worcestershire and the surrounding counties. I have always regarded myself as a country auctioneer and certainly not an expert. Over the past twenty-five years I have met some colourful characters with fascinating possessions: these stories are based on just some of them.

Lot 1

The Man with a Tin Leg

My entry into the auctioneering world was not the most orthodox; certainly my post-school qualifications were not especially relevant to my chosen career. That in itself is another story – I started out as an auctioneer's assistant when some three months earlier I had left the best PE college in the country armed with a certificate to enable me to teach PE and geography. The fact that I never did so must be a huge relief to a whole generation of children. I had always had an interest in antiques and fine art. I think living on a smallholding with my parents, where I was surrounded by the archaic, had stimulated a natural interest in all things old – in particular, things that stemmed from the rural way of life through several generations. However, at eighteen playing cricket and rugby seemed more appealing so off I went to Loughborough College of Physical Education.

My first boss was Major Ernest Edward Foley Rayer, MBE, TD, FRICS, CAAV. In simple terms, as well as being a Member of the British Empire, he had been awarded the Territorial Army Decoration, was a Fellow of the Royal Institution of Chartered Surveyors and a member of the Central Association of Agricultural Valuers. He was a unique character and a man respected by all. When my father's insurance broker heard that I was about to go and work for the major, he told me that I would never make any real money as 'Ted was far too honest ever to make a fortune.' That struck me as being a cast-iron testimonial. He was an ex-army man of about sixty-five who had lost his leg in the Second World War. The amputation was very high and for a time there was some question as to whether he would survive or not. Not that he, apparently, was in any doubt. The determination that enabled him to come through those early days after his operation saw him learn in the years after the war to cycle, swim and ride horses. He was a keen huntsman, a hobby that his wife was aware of in passing, not realising how actively he pursued it. Mr Rayer – this was how I always addressed him, even after some fifteen years as colleagues when he asked me to call him Ted; I only managed to do that two years after he died – used to keep his horse at one friend's farm and his horse box at another. He would leave home on the pretext of going to follow the hunt and then deviate to collect his horse and horse box for a day of his chosen sport.

This subterfuge worked quite well for some time, until an unhappy incident alerted his wife to his double life. Mr Rayer was not the prettiest of riders, resembling a rather large sack of potatoes in the saddle. On the fateful day Mr Rayer's grey mare went to jump a large hawthorn hedge but was all wrong in stride for take-off. The horse went one way, the saddle another and 'EEFR', or the 'Galloping Major' as he was known in some circles, another. The problem was that his tin leg went a fourth, which resulted in one of the lady hunt followers becoming hysterical, as she hadn't realised the leg was artificial. The lady was an acquaintance of Mrs Rayer but did not know the major at all and she was thus unaware of his disability. Apparently when she came round she was rushed home and took delight in telephoning the major's wife to tell her exactly what had happened. When Mr Rayer eventually returned, with the aid of two brooms as makeshift crutches, Mrs Rayer greeted him with a formidable lecture on topics ranging from 'the appropriate time to grow up' to 'the need to take responsibilities seriously'.

Mr Rayer was stubborn, cantankerous, utterly professional and a complete gentleman. He was also a dreadful timekeeper, which resulted in another of his nicknames, 'Ten o'clock Ted', because that was the time he normally arrived at his nine o'clock appointments.

His shocking memory and total inability to keep track of time led me into a predicament on my first Monday at work back in November 1976.

Having realised that teaching was not for me I had decided that auctioneering was to be the chosen route. At that time most auctioneering practices were multi-disciplined, involved with estate and land agency as well as the various forms of auctioneering. My attempts to find work in my new career resulted in numerous firms politely declining my offer to assist and improve their businesses with my presence. I had had an interview with Mr Rayer late on the previous Friday afternoon. It hadn't seemed like an interview; we had simply sat down and talked for about an hour and a half. I was surprised because he seemed really interested in me and what I was doing and why I wanted to become an auctioneer. He was one of the county's leading agricultural auctioneers and valuers, and the firm had sixteen offices in Worcestershire, Herefordshire and Gloucestershire. It was a general practice business involved in the sale of houses, professional work and land agency, as well as running two livestock markets and, of course, antique sales. As a trainee with the firm I would have to learn about all these disciplines. Mr Rayer introduced me to his colleagues in the office; one striking character among them was a certain J. Clifford Atkins, whose wing I was also to fall under in years to come.

At the end of my interview with Mr Rayer he offered me a job and told me that I should be in the office on Monday morning wearing a pin-stripe suit and to make sure I had a pair of wellies to hand as I was never to know when I might need them. I therefore duly appeared in the office, only to be a little put out by Mr Rayer not remembering who I was. I was absolutely resplendent in a brand-new pin-stripe suit with a pair of shiny new wellies, which I had had to borrow money from my father to buy. As the years passed I never ceased to wonder why I should have been told to buy that suit – in twenty-five years of knowing Mr Rayer I never saw him in one. He always wore a tweed jacket, with waistcoat in the winter, and good strong trousers. The jacket and waistcoat always looked as if they had been retrieved from a bonfire: Mr Rayer had smoked a pipe for nearly half a century when I met him and yet he still hadn't mastered the art of lighting his pipe without the resultant sparks scorching and burning holes in his clothes.

So, as I said, when I walked into the office for that first morning's work he simply could not remember that he had offered me a job. However, like everything, he took it in his stride, told me it was market day in the city and that I should walk to the market and help draw the sheep. Well, the market was only a few hundred yards away and the thought of a restful day drawing pictures of sheep I found quite appealing. Quite why I would be doing so, I couldn't imagine, but I didn't want to disturb Mr Rayer's good humour by asking questions. To my horror I found that drawing sheep meant climbing into a pen full of the woolly but suddenly intimidating animals and lifting them into various other pens until they were sorted by size. In my brand-new pin-stripe suit. To add to my woes it had just started to rain and I was at the soggy, mucky end of the wretched animals.

The other market drovers and trainee auctioneers wore old clothes and thorn-proof, waxed leggings. The local farming fraternity could not quite believe what they saw in front of them. I come from a farming family and I didn't hear the last of this for years. Indeed for some of the locals I think I passed into folklore.

After my baptism at the rear end of the sheep I kept my head down in the office. I was the butt of jokes and leg-pulling by all and the other trainees were particularly sharp with their repartee. The pecking order among the three of us trainees was simple: I was at the bottom of the ladder by dint of the fact that I had been with the firm the shortest time. The others worked for the various partners and senior valuers but I was specifically assigned to Mr Rayer. His team comprised his secretary and me. She was a lovely girl, if a little scatty, and we shared a room on the first floor of the offices in Worcester. Her finest attribute to me seemed to be an almost telepathic understanding of what her employer wanted. The intercom system in the office resembled those you see in Second World War submarine films – a precarious system of pipes with whistles and bangs. Mr Rayer, to whom this was all new-fangled technology, would bellow, because that's what he thought you had to do, 'Please bring in doings' file!' down his end of the pipe. Who doings was, and where and what his file looked like I had no idea. When it was my turn to take doings' file in I invariably got the wrong doings; when it was her turn she was always spot-on.

The original firm had been founded in 1791 and Mr Rayer's family had run it for many generations, dealing similarly with generations of the same clients. Bentley, Hobbs and Mytton was the firm's name, and the Hobbses were the link to Mr Rayer on his mother's side of the family; the Bentleys and Myttons were long since gone.

I used to enjoy going out with him to visit the farming fraternity in the county. His driving was legendary throughout the area and had been known to reduce previous trainees to gibbering wrecks. His car was a ten-year-old Triumph, 'Thunderbird IV', which had an interior resembling the pocket of a rather naughty twelve-year-old schoolboy: conkers, paper, stubby pencils, penknives, string and the like everywhere. It looked as if it had played a part in the chariot scene in the film *Ben Hur*: every panel had a dent or a bump where Mr Rayer hadn't so much had an accident as wandered into something, be it another car, tree or – in one notable incident – a cow. The firm used to conduct wine auctions and Mr Rayer's horse box was used to convey the cases of wine to the saleroom. One young man by the name of Simon was so nervous of his boss's driving that he chose to travel in the trailer rather than in the car with Mr Rayer. This may have seemed a wise decision until, while taking, probably too quickly, a left-hand bend, the groom's door at the front of the horse box flew open and deposited young Simon and some equally young claret on the side of the road. Apparently he never came back to work again.

During our trips, Mr Rayer would regale me with information about the local families and their histories. The only problem was that he used to get very animated during these chats. This, while he was driving, was not good for my nerves, and when these tales coincided with his pipe-lighting routine I really was on the edge of the seat. Perhaps the worst occasion was when driving along a country lane in Herefordshire as he told me about a farm we had passed. He decided to turn around in his seat as he described a particular field of cattle he had valued. Just before he began this story he had started to light his pipe and there was the usual flurry of sparks and burning embers. The problem got worse when the bowl of Mr Rayer's pipe, which was held to the stem by tape, fell out and landed in his lap, depositing red-hot ash everywhere. Not unnaturally, I was showing a little concern, which turned to panic when I saw a tractor with a large roller behind it coming towards us and occupying the whole road. The point of impact was now surely only feet away, so I closed my eyes and got as close to the crash position that they advise in aeroplanes as I could. I was aware of my head rotating through about 100 degrees and back again. Still no bang. After a time I opened my eyes: the road ahead of us was clear and I turned round to see the tractor behind us. Mr Rayer was still in full flow about the magnificent herd of pedigree Hereford cattle we had passed, seemingly totally unaware of the doom that might have just fleetingly passed us. How we had avoided a major prang I will never know.

One of my roles in the office was to make appointments for Mr Rayer and to accompany him to look at furniture that clients were thinking of including in one of the firm's future sales. I had made such a date for us to travel out to a lovely timbered village some four miles outside the city. The local lord of the manor owned the bulk of the village and he had steadfastly refused to see the village overdeveloped as so many have been. Consequently property values were high and the village was a desirable place to live. I therefore reasoned that anything to be sold from a house in this village must be good. I was quite looking forward to the call. I told Mr Rayer that I thought we had a good appointment and off we set with me in charge of navigation.

We stopped at a T-junction in the city waiting to turn left. I was pleased we had come to a halt because coming up the street was a huge lorry and I did not fancy our chances against it. Mr Rayer sat talking to me about nothing in particular and then to my horror pushed the automatic gear selector from 'P' for park to 'D' for drive. This would have been a chancy manoeuvre even in a normal car but Mr Rayer's car had a mind of its own. You would engage drive and wait for something to happen. The engine would rev strongly and still nothing would happen until, suddenly, there would be a bang as cogs seemed to drop into place and the car would lurch off at its own steady pace, with noise inversely proportional to speed. The trouble was you never knew when the bang and forward motion would occur, so pulling out from a junction, which could be a bit tricky anyway, was, under these circumstances, a nightmare. The road the lorry was travelling along was of the two-lane type leading up to some traffic lights. The lorry was in the left-hand lane and we cut it up a treat; it was a miracle that the poor chap managed to stop. When the lorry driver had recovered his senses, he got his truck to within six inches of Mr Rayer's rear bumper, pressed the horn very loudly and flashed a myriad of lights that lit up the old Triumph like Blackpool pleasure beach.

I was sliding down the seat trying hard to look like it had nothing to do with me when I glanced behind and noticed that the lorry had pulled over to the right-hand lane. I believe we had in rowing terms about half a canvas lead on him when Mr Rayer obviously felt that narrowly escaping death once in the day was not enough. To my horror, without any signal, we pulled from the left-hand lane into the right-hand lane and cut the trucker up for a second time. We got the same horn and headlamp treatment. As we were approaching the traffic lights they changed from green to amber. This was a relief, as I knew Mr Rayer would not stop and the lorry driver would.

My life began to pass before my eyes as Mr Rayer did, in fact, halt; in all the years I travelled with him it was the only time I had ever known him to stop on amber. I heard the air brakes go on the lorry, and the lorry door open and slam shut. Mr Rayer, completely oblivious to anything that had happened since the T-junction, decided it was time to light his pipe so there were smoke, sparks and ashes blowing everywhere. I sensed a figure walking up to the driver's window of the Triumph. The lorry driver then launched into my employer in a way that was quite educational. Mr Rayer just looked at him and said, 'Bloody sauce,' and pushed the gear selector from P to D, with no regard for the fact that the lights were still on red. The old 'Thunderbird IV' for once moved instantly, leaving the hapless lorry driver standing in the middle of the road, giving a severe ticking-off to no one in particular.

I was relieved when we finally got out of the city but confused when I told Mr Rayer that we should head west and he turned to the east. I nervously questioned this only to be told that he had another little job to do on the way. I didn't think it was my place to mention that as we were travelling in the exact opposite direction it hardly seemed on the way. We eventually found ourselves at the home of one Dickie Wilton. Dickie worked at the firm's livestock markets and the little job was to discuss the entries for the next cattle market. As this should take only a few minutes I sat in the car and waited – and waited. Some twenty minutes later Mr Rayer made his way back to the car and we set off again. We were now about thirty minutes late and I just hoped our clients there would understand.

As we pulled into the village Mr Rayer asked me for the exact address. I suddenly realised that our call was not at one of the more desirable cottages but one of the ex-council houses on the road leaving the village. As we drove round the corner on the way out of the village my heart sank. Parked outside one of the houses was a lorry painted in the same livery as the one we had had our difficulties with earlier. But this surely couldn't be the same one. As we slowly drove up to the houses the horrible suspicion dawned that we were indeed about to be reintroduced to our earlier antagonist. My nerve ends were now at breaking point; Mr Rayer naturally was totally oblivious to all this. We walked up the path and knocked at the front door. To my relief a lady answered and welcomed us in to look at her antique dining-room suite. Well, it was 'Elizabethan' but unfortunately from the reign of Elizabeth II and not much older than about 1955. Mr Rayer sympathetically told the lady that there was not much demand for these and they normally made about £50. By now I was hopping from foot to foot as if I had some incontinence problem, trying to will us out of there before the man of the house appeared, in case it was the same driver we had encountered earlier.

'I'd better just go and get my husband and see what he wants to do.' My heart sank. Mr Rayer, of course, had no inkling of the possible looming confrontation. The door opened and in walked our lorry driver. Before he could say anything Mr Rayer repeated that there wasn't much call for these suites and it would only make a few tens of pounds.

It was quite interesting to watch as the trucker's skin took on the colour of a rich Victoria plum. Rage was about to explode out of him like an erupting volcano. During the next few seconds, which seemed an eternity, I was unsure what sort of assault – physical or verbal – was about to ensue.

'Get out of my bloody house,' eventually spewed forth. 'Just get out. *Now!*'

I thought discretion was the better part of valour and guided Mr Rayer at once to the front door. As we walked down the path to the car Mr Rayer said, 'You know, Philip, I realise not everyone thinks my valuations are right, but no one has ever reacted like that before.'

Lot 2

A Stubborn Cow

I now look back on those early days in the market with the major fondly. They were, quite simply, fun. But then in memories of childhood holidays it never rains. It was like that with my first job; however, in reality it was not all beer and skittles. At that time – we had just celebrated the Queen's Silver Jubilee – the firm ran a weekly market in Worcester and a monthly market in Bromyard. Bromyard was a small town about fifteen miles due west of Worcester, which was christened by those in the office with the most apt nickname of Dodge City – while I don't think anyone was ever shot there, it did seem to sum up the general goings-on in the market rather well. As the trainee, my job was to get to the market first and make sure everything was ready for the sale to start at ten o'clock.

Two men who had more experience at markets than I'd had hot dinners helped me. One was a Welshman, rather unimaginatively named Dai, and the other was the great Dickie Wilton. Dickie was a legend throughout the farming fraternity in the county. He was an honest, likeable and thoroughly charming individual who could smell a deal or a tip from twenty paces away. Dickie was always armed with a clipboard and gave the impression he was busy. I'm sure he would have confused many a time and motion study man, but no one was really sure what he actually did. He was employed by the firm to see that everything at the market ran smoothly. This included making sure that all the stock were in the right pens and that all the farmers who were selling their stock were happy. Dickie normally achieved these goals by delegation, until the time came for the happy seller or buyer to part with a tip. Then Dickie came into his own, as he managed to guide the helpless farmer client away from all the other staff and explained how the only reason such a good price had been achieved, or, if he was talking to the buyer, the reason why the animal had been so cheap was solely due to Dickie's efforts. We all knew Dickie did this but still thought the world of him.

Dai's job was to get there early enough in the morning to help me prepare the office. This was always difficult for Dai until he had had his breakfast. It would have been impossible for anybody else after indulging in Dai's early morning snap, which was a large jug of scrumpy cider that had bits floating in it and a wedge of cheese so strong that mouth ulcers became a formality. He used to arrive armed with a large, thick, broad-headed broom ready to sweep the office floor. As the market was only monthly the accumulation was always a good, thick one. Dai and the broom didn't so much collect the dust as redistribute it, so after about fifteen minutes it would look as if the entire Sioux nation had ridden through the office. Having achieved this, Dai would abandon his broom to light the gas lamps. I don't recall whose job it was to bring new mantles, which were always needed – probably mine – but someone always forgot. This meant that, after being lit, the lamps roared like inverted bunsen burners, which had dire effects on the coiffured hair of the two ladies who came over from Worcester for the day to take the cash. They were both about sixty and had been christened 'Hinge and Bracket' by me (for readers too young to know, Hinge and Bracket were two elderly, distinguished ladies from a comedy television series, played by two young men). Neither referred to the other by anything other than their surname, they both drank lemon tea and they smoked like troopers (which fatally took its toll on both of them).

Once the office was prepared my next task was to book in the cattle. In this I was 'helped' by two of Dai's mates, 'Derek the Digger Dumper Driver' and 'Jack Mash'. These were two Irishmen and while the reason for the first's nickname was obvious, I have no idea how the second came about. Derek was reputedly responsible for the construction of more motorway miles than any other Irishman in the country. Jack Mash didn't seem to have any proper job but, in common with Derek and Dai, was able to consume vast quantities of alcohol. Like Hinge and Bracket, they were about sixty but while Dai and Derek carried size-able corporations above the waistline, Jack Mash was a wiry soul who seemed to weigh no more than six stone. This also repre-sented the volume he was able to consume in cider. All three of them appeared at the market scrupulously clean, but in clothes that dated back to their army days in the late forties. They had in common a complexion of a rich ruddy-brown colour.

The market was very small and never had much stock but it still used to take me hours to book it in: this meant I had to record the name and address of the farmer and the minimum price he would take, together with any other details. Farming family I might come from, but I couldn't tell bullock from cow from heifer. I used to spend what seemed like hours on all fours trying to work out the sex of the beast in front of me, and whether the vet had left its reproductive areas the way the good Lord intended them to be. Once that was more or less successfully accomplished, everything would be ready for the off – unless a lot of rain fell in between monthly markets. If it did, the scales that weighed the cattle used to flood below ground where the weighing mechanism was. I was the lad in the firm, and if anything ever went wrong, it was always the lad's job to fix it. It was therefore my duty to bale out this chamber. The stagnant water had an aroma all of its own, which was bad enough, but I used to dread a really cold spell which meant the water in the chamber froze solid. In that case I'd have to boil water in an old gas-lit boiler at the back of the office, and use this to try to unfreeze the flood. The scales at the market were always thoroughly and accurately inspected by the weights and measures man, but they always seemed more like a basis of negotiation to me.

When the market had finished, the elders of the firm retired to the pub, which opened all day, to have a drink with their clients, and everybody else went back to Worcester. The elders were normally led by Mr Rayer and included the senior managers and the other assistant auctioneers. It most definitely did not include the young trainee – me. The after-market drink was important to the firm as it was seen as an opportunity to get a closer to clients who might have something to sell a little more profitable to the firm than a three-year-old cow. As the lad I had to be last to leave the market. This used to become fairly tedious because the buyers always stayed in the pub for what seemed like eternity. It was my job with Dai, Derek the Digger Dumper Driver and Jack Mash to put the cattle and sheep into pens allocated by the new owners and then to hose down the remaining pens ready for next month's market. This would not have been too onerous a task for my three little helpers and me. However, two words rendered this a one-man job: 'pub' and 'open'. The idea of a career path didn't seem of much interest to them but since I was anxious not to blot my copybook, I would never desert my post. So they left me to get on with the jobs. The strange thing was that I never felt used in any way at all; they even asked me if I minded before they went.

It was after the market that Dickie Wilton came into his own, striding around with his clipboard, looking for all the world as if he were checking everything was in order. He would always stop and help me out, for which I was grateful but soon realised that, because he didn't drink, this was a marketing opportunity. He would sell eggs and anything else he had bought or grown to those leaving the pub. Dickie couldn't afford to have his judgement impaired by alcohol when there were important deals to be done. I often watched him in action with these hardened farmers, who were like lambs to the slaughter with Dickie. His skills were really under-utilised; he could have sold ice to Eskimos. I well remember what I thought was his greatest deal. Eric Jennings was one of the area's largest poultry farmers. The number of chickens he had in the huge sheds on his farm was a subject of wonder across the county, hotly debated by all. Eric had been in the pub and, having had perhaps one more whisky than he should, wobbled out into the market. Dickie moved in, and before Eric knew what was happening he had bought a tray of two dozen eggs at a little over market rate. The story does not quite end there, in that legend has it that the eggs had been bought by Dickie that morning from Eric's farm shop. Dickie was good company and I was pleased to call him a friend. In quieter moments we used to sit down in the office and talk about how auctioneering had changed over the years.

The very nature of business meant there could not be as much trust as there had once been. This was a time when farming was going through huge changes. Some farmers were now borrowing more money from banks and finance houses to fund bigger machinery, more stock and acquire more land. The motto seemed very much to be that bigger is better. The hefty repayments were beginning to result in cash flow problems and the inevitable bouncing cheques that accompanied them. What made things worse was that many buyers, rather than attending the market themselves, would have a representative bidding on their behalf. Sometimes this individual would be bidding on behalf of more than one person, which meant his resources would often be over-stretched. On one notorious occasion an individual representing several buyers ran up credit in excess of £10,000 at various local markets. In those days this represented the value of a decent town house. It may seem inconceivable that someone should be allowed to run up debts of that level, but such an agent carrying many bids was a powerful man at a market and his promise to pay would not have been taken lightly. Unfortunately when the buyers paid him, he did not pass the funds on. This particular episode caused a lot of heartache and changes in policy, for a man's word could no longer be taken as his bond.

Quiet moments, however, were few and far between. Usually, while my colleagues were drinking, we were hard at it; me trying to make sure all was in order, and Dickie doing his deals. One particular afternoon found us both on the ramp of a cattle lorry attempting to get a particularly stubborn steer into the truck. It had got halfway up the ramp and simply refused to go any further. There was no reason for this; it just stopped. Many people credit animals with thought processes. I don't think that's the case, although this particular beast seemed hell-bent on doing the exact opposite of what we wanted. The more we pushed, the more firmly it seemed rooted to the spot. Dickie told me that we should both put our shoulders behind its rear knees and push, him on one side and me on the other. It was a bit like second row forwards at rugby. I wasn't too sure about this but Dickie was adamant that this was a method that never failed. I must admit to feeling slightly vulnerable for two reasons. First, if my new bovine friend were to get a little unfriendly I would be within range of a good kick. Second, and I'm not sure this didn't worry me more, if the brute did not have complete control of its bowels, I really was in pole position. Those of you who have been around cattle will know that a cowpat when first deposited is normally of a very runny consistency.

After a few seconds' pushing with no discernible result the beast took its revenge, targeting me. It was a strange sensation, not unlike standing under a mildly warm shower where someone has mixed too much wallpaper paste with the water. Luckily I had a market smock coat on which took the brunt of the deluge. Dickie, to his credit, did not even smile. I have to admit if the boot had been on the other foot I would have been in fits. But the situation had still not changed: one immovable object on the ramp of a cattle truck. Dickie disappeared for a short while, telling me not to go anywhere. I thought this was rather unnecessary advice given the state I was in. After a while he reappeared with a length of thick nylon hose piping about two inches in diameter.

'Here, Phil, I'll push him from behind and you give him a tap on the arse with this.' Well, I didn't like the sound of this: first, I wasn't too keen on hitting animals and, second, I thought of the reaction I'd got from it previously just for pushing. Lord knows what it would do if I started to whack it. But Dickie once again was adamant.

'One, two, three, *now!*' he shouted. Rather wimpishly I brought down the three-foot length of pipe.

'No, no, no!' yelled Dickie. 'You've really got to give him some – it won't hurt him.'

This pantomime continued with my strokes gradually getting firmer and Dickie beginning to lose his patience – with me, not with the beast. By this time quite a crowd had developed to see what was going on but, interestingly enough, no one offered to help. I decided I would give it my all in one last effort.

'Come on, Phil, one, two, three, now!'

So I did.

The pipe came whistling down in my hand. It had just passed the point of no return when the animal suddenly started to move into the truck. My joy as I realised I was not going to have to hit it again turned to horror when, as the animal moved, the balding pate of Dickie came into view and replaced it as a target. The sound as it hit him on the head was like a rifle going off. Dickie went down as if he had been shot. There was a gasp from the sizeable audience we had now gathered. I could hear mutterings: should they call an ambulance, would Dickie's widow cope, and what sort of prison term would I get for manslaughter. This was not at all comforting, I rather selfishly thought, ignoring Dickie's plight. How was I going to explain this at an inquest? After a while, with me shaking him, Dickie started to groan; obviously he wasn't dead and the charge I would now be facing was only grievous bodily harm. After a time Dickie got to his feet.

'Bloody hell,' he said, 'I'm not sure you're cut out for this market work.'

Was he right? Was it time to try to develop

my career in a different area of the business? After all, antiques didn't do what this cow had done to me, or even kick you. Maybe they were a better option than ill-tempered livestock.

Lot 3

The Bull with a Sweet Tooth

It was a Monday morning and I had been working with Mr Rayer for some time; I was trying – if you'll pardon the pun – somewhat sheepishly to hide from the severe leg-pulling that was rife in the office. My suit-wearing appearance in the livestock market on my first day, struggling with wet sheep, was still the subject of much hilarity.

The intercom buzzed in my office; it was a sound that struck terror in the heart as it meant my new boss was trying to get hold of me. He would bellow his instruction down the system; through the resulting cacophony of hissing and shouting, I eventually translated my employer's wishes.

'Philip, you'd better pop over to doings and help lot up Saturday's sale.'

As I left the office I wondered uneasily what lotting up a sale entailed and, more urgently, who on earth 'doings' was. (Every item in an auction sale is described as a lot and is given a number starting at 'Lot 1', moving on until all the items to be sold are identified with a number. It sounds very simple and should be so – except that none of EEFR's jobs ever were.)

Mr Rayer's secretary was out for the day but eventually Hinge and Bracket, the other two secretaries, came to my assistance. Doings, in this instance, was a fourth-generation farmer by the name of Gilbert Nash who bred some of the best cattle in the district on a farm of about 200 acres, equidistant between Worcester and Hereford. His sons, like many of their generation, had decided that a life on the land was not for them and Mr Nash had reached the conclusion that now was the time to sell while land prices were so buoyant. The firm had already sold the farm and now all the farm machinery and implements, together with the household furniture, had to go; also the pedigree Hereford bull. I set off with a map on the passenger seat of my father's car which I was borrowing in the short term as I had no other means of transport. I entered the small village, knowing only roughly the whereabouts of the farm, and assumed I would soon come across this Saturday's sale venue. I spent twenty fruitless minutes driving around in ever decreasing circles with no sign of the Nash farm. The village in those days was totally off the tourist trail, but bizarrely was home to a small shop and the post office that sold home-made toffee. An ideal place, I thought, to call in and check on the whereabouts of the Nash family and also to sample the local delicacy.

The lady serving in the shop was about sixty-five and it was certainly evident that she enjoyed her job – eating the produce. She was not square, but more of a sideways rectangle, about five feet two inches tall and, I swear, five feet six inches wide. Her cheeks were as red as two local apples and her clothes had perhaps once better fitted a less portly frame. She wore a bright red knitted cardigan with gaping holes on the elbows and a long blue and green tartan skirt that was more Hereford Home Guard than Scotland's Black Watch. I am not really sure why, but she also wore shiny wellingtons that looked as if they'd never seen the outside of her shop; they were almost as pristine as my first day market wellies. She was the type of lady that my grandmother always described as, 'An ideal farmer's wife; she's a real good worker.' I always understood this to mean that a lack of good looks was more than made up for by the ability to move hundredweight sacks of corn on each shoulder.

'This'll put hairs on yer chest,' she said, picking up a small paper bag of home-made toffee. Looking at her chin I could see it wasn't just the chest it worked on.

'Only the best gredients from me 'usband's farm fer me secrit recipe – 'anded down over the generashuns.'

She offered me a small sample from the packet she was holding. I couldn't help but notice that, of all the unevenly sized home-made sweets, I got the smallest while she unwrapped three of the larger ones for herself. As soon as I popped it into my mouth I thanked the Lord all my teeth were my own, for those chews would have wreaked havoc with the unsuspecting denture-wearer. In fact any loose tooth or filling was in grave danger of being ripped from its socket.

'Oi rusally get frew a frare frew packits miself jurin a day,' I think she said through a mouthful of what I was discovering to be an incredibly rich, sweet and extremely adhesive toffee. It was lovely, but how she could eat the quantity she appeared to was beyond me. 'Chewy' only went halfway to describing the substance, which was like Araldite.

'Oi was a slip of a girl when I marrid me 'usband but 'e likes 'em with a bit of meat on.'

Her toffees had obviously done the trick and her husband must have been a very happy man. I was still struggling with the pea-sized lump I had been offered when it became apparent that she had polished off her three. Her jaws were surely like industrial grinders.

'Ow meny yud like?' was her closing sales pitch; I thought it would be rude not to have two bags. They would last me months and should prove invaluable as an emergency repair kit if I ever got a hole in my exhaust.

As I walked towards the door I remembered why I'd called in in the first place. I stopped and asked the genial shopkeeper if she knew where Gilbert Nash lived and back came the reply: ''E's me 'usband.'

Relieved, I asked for directions.

Her reply ominously started with, 'Well, it's simple really...'

Experience has taught me that any answer beginning like that usually requires a PhD to understand. One of my many failings is the habit of asking someone for directions and then not listening to the reply. Ridiculous, true, but I'm sure I am not the only one. This was one of those occasions, and the route sounded like the sort of treasure hunt in which everyone gets lost. I thought I had got the rough gist of her instructions, however, and was about to leave when she asked why I wanted to know. I explained that I was Mr Rayer's new trainee and was about to say that I was to help lot up the sale when she burst into fits of laughter.

''U the one with the soot in the ship pens?' She chortled. News obviously travelled like wildfire in these parts.

Off I went, marvelling as I reached the door that the dear lady, who was now roaring with hysterics, was still able to feed another handful of her toffees into her mouth at the same time.

Right out of the shop, left past the telephone box, bear left again past the bungalow with the hedge – but not the one with the fence or I would go hopelessly wrong – down through the ford, then drop down to the right past the field with a bull in it. Bull? I didn't much like the sound of that. Apparently his name was Hector; he was to be sold on Saturday and was really friendly. 'Bull' and 'friendly' had always seemed a contradiction in terms to me and I remained to be convinced otherwise.

The road had been gradually getting rougher; by now it had grass growing in the middle of its single track. I knew all too painfully that if you hit a road like this you might not be seen again for days. I reached the farm gate; it was of the type that had been booby-trapped to repel all unwanted visitors who had not been issued with instructions as to how it should be opened. I lacked these instructions. I opened the gate gingerly, thinking, not unreasonably, that it would swing open on its hinges. I was wrong: it dropped to the ground like a stone, slowing down only when it struck my leg just below the knee. Fortunately my mother was still trying to get the smell of muck from my suit trousers after the sheep episode, otherwise they would have been ripped to shreds. A lesson learned: I was wearing a pair of old cords that had seen better days and now took on an interesting mottled colour as blood seeped through. I am ashamed to admit the air turned a similarly interesting blue as I let forth a stream of fairly educational expletives.

Finally I pulled into the farmyard to find Dai, Derek the Digger Dumper Driver and Jack Mash busy doing not very much at all, an art form they had honed to perfection. The likeable trio were waiting for Mr Rayer, who was travelling – thankfully – by independent means, to come and issue his instructions as to how he wanted the sale lotted up. Instead of kicking our heels, pending the arrival of our boss, we decided to wander around and see exactly what the job entailed. We walked, or in my case limped, out of the yard and saw that the fields inclined on both sides; the farmhouse and buildings nestled in a natural valley. The open barn on the side nearest the farm-house was the implement store. I peered in. There were tractors, engines, ploughs and other machinery that looked as old as the hills. I was staggered by the sheer volume of it all; it was piled high from floor to ceiling.

Mr Nash was a man who never threw anything away just in case, one day, it might come in useful.

As we walked around the corner we saw him coming towards us. The Nashes must have looked an odd couple together. He was about six feet four inches tall and could not have weighed more than ten and a half stone. He sported a 'Fred Dibnah' type flat cap and overalls as worn by old steam train drivers. Both the cap and overalls were covered in oil and axle grease but, strangely, appeared otherwise clean; no doubt they had been his favourite garments for the last thirty years. He had a thin face with huge ginger mutton-chop sideburns and on his feet wore 'toe-tector' boots; the fabric had worn away to reveal shiny steel toecaps.

By now Mr Rayer had arrived to join us and we walked out into what had once been an old apple orchard and was now a scrapheap. There were some fifteen huge piles of scrap and derelict machines heaped around the tree trunks. As we wandered up to each mound of metal our client suddenly lunged forward and kicked the pile as hard as he could, occasionally letting out a yelp as his toes crunched into the rusting mass. None of my colleagues seemed to notice anything amiss, but I couldn't help asking what on earth he was doing. He explained it was his method of gauging the calibre of the

45

scrap – the more it hurt the better the quality. Each pile of scrap contained old parts once belonging to all sorts of weird and wonderful engines and machines.

Then we walked back up the track to the gate through which I had first driven to the farm. I was starting to feel a little nervous; this was getting a mite too close to Hector country. I am an animal lover but always feel more comfortable when there is a considerable distance between me and them, ideally with a large hedge or fence as added security. Alarm bells rang out when Gilbert Nash told us that he had sold all the rest of his stock at market but had decided not to take Hector as he was a tad frisky at the time. Terrific news.

I had soon learned that one of my duties when out with my new boss was to act as his minder. Minder in the sense that I was there to pick him up every time he fell over; and fall over he did, with alarming regularity. I would leap in to help him up, or, if I was quicker off the mark, try to stop him from falling over. Given that he would never head for a gate or gap in a hedge, but would try to climb over the obstacle like any able-bodied person, meant that he spent a fair amount of time on his backside. His response as I leaped to his aid was fairly predictable: 'I haven't brought you along to help me up – you're here to try and learn something.'

As we approached Hector I'm afraid my nerves got the better of me and I started to desert my boss and drop back a pace or two. I had no intention of getting any nearer to this two-ton, 'frisky' beefburger than I had to. As Mr Rayer and Gilbert Nash got closer to the damn thing it started to paw the ground; surely that meant an attack was imminent?

'He's a baby, young man,' Gilbert called in my direction.

I was quite happy to take his word in the matter but Mr Rayer seemed to think that it was vital to my continuing education to get as close to Hector as possible. Cowardice dictated it was time for me to slip gently back towards the house.

'I'd better go and see what there is to be done inside,' I hastily exclaimed, feeling rather guilty, as I could hear Mr Rayer shouting something as I disappeared out of earshot. I'm afraid I kept going.

I soon began to wish I had stayed outside.

When I made my way through the front door the state of the house was as bad as the outbuildings: nothing had ever been thrown away and it was all in a tangled mess, just like the inside of the implement shed. Mrs Nash was still at the shop, so I was left to wander around on my own. All I could see were mountains of what, to my untrained eyes, seemed like unsaleable tat. With more experience in my new career the panic bells would have started to ring: an auctioneer with a tin leg, Dai and his two mates, and a twenty-one-year-old who was completely wet behind the ears had five days to sort this stuff out for an auction sale on Saturday.

After twenty minutes of me not actually achieving anything, Mr Rayer appeared to 'help' me. Apparently, some weeks ago back in the office, he had produced a catalogue of the lots for sale and all we had to do was attach the numbers from the list he had produced to the right article in the sale. Simple. Well, in theory yes, but practice was another thing. The trouble was, as far as I could see, Mr Rayer appeared to have brought a catalogue that related to a totally different farm; I couldn't marry up anything. My boss was undeterred.

'Lot 1 goes on the doings over there.'

Oh great, that's really helpful, I thought, struggling to find any doings that resembled his description. Lot 1 took this dynamic duo about fifteen minutes to locate and put a number on. At this rate we would need five weeks, not five days to sort it all out. Eventually we got a 'system' going, as Mr Rayer put it; I have to admit we did speed up, but I wasn't sure whether we were both working to the same system. His sole instructions were for me to find a 'doings' and as yet my telepathic skills were not quite as highly tuned as they might have been. We carried on until about seven o'clock in the evening – with Mr Rayer you worked if it was light and you sometimes worked if it was dark – and eventually made our way outside.

Astonishingly, we appeared to have made some progress. To my amazement, the Celtic trio were making great strides in sorting things outside. Armed with a tractor, they had managed to drag a fair amount of the machinery out into the fields. They were fortunate; they had neither a catalogue nor a system from Mr Rayer to work to. I didn't want to be a killjoy, but looking at Mr Rayer's previously prepared list, it occurred to me that none of the items they had moved were in any order at all. Still, I was sure my boss, with all his strategic military experience, would have a plan whereby everything would fall miraculously into place. It was time to go home and I arranged to meet Mr Rayer at seven thirty in the morning at the office; my father needed his car so I had no option but to beg a lift to the farm with the boss after being dropped off.

I was at the office the next morning about fifteen minutes early, only to find my employer already at his desk preparing another valuation he had been working on. His office was a time warp: there were old prints on the walls that showed Worcester in the eighteenth and nineteenth centuries, and a wonderful

Regency rosewood bookcase stuffed with books and journals covering a multitude of topics. His mahogany partner's desk was littered with files that could have dated back a hundred years or more and, as I later found out, some of them actually did. I suggested, respectfully, that perhaps we should move on as I felt we had a long day ahead of us at the Nashes. I offered to carry his briefcase, which held the all-important pre-prepared catalogue, only to be told, 'Very kind, Philip, but I can carry my own case. You're here to try and learn something.'

At which point, he opened the bookcase door and got out a book. He told me it would be useful and informative and recommended that I should read it. The book was all about auction law and practices. I chuckled when I eventually looked at it later on that evening and discovered it was nearly eighty years out of date; to him it was probably exciting new stuff.

Normally I let others precede me down the office stairs. With Mr Rayer I led the way as I reasoned that if he fell I would at least cushion him.

We reached the car park at the rear of the office without mishap and found Thunderbird IV, Mr Rayer's old Triumph. I got into the car first as I did not want to offend this fiercely independent man again by offering to help him. Off we set and it soon occurred to me that Mr Rayer must have known quite a number of folk in the county; as we left the city drivers in almost every other car we met flashed their lights and waved at us. I found it quite comforting to be in the employment of such a well-known and respected man. However I began to sense that it probably wasn't just friendliness when a certain well-known lorry haulage firm from Cumbria did the same.

Naturally Mr Rayer had noticed very little of all this and I felt it prudent to suggest that we pull over and check whether a wheel was about to drop off. After about a mile we came to a suitable gateway where I suggested we stop; he ignored this and drove on, instead pulling on to the side of the road on a particularly bad bend. I hoped that whatever our problem was it was not going to take too long to sort out before we caused a serious accident. It didn't: as I got out of the car I saw Mr Rayer's briefcase on the roof above the driver's seat. He was remarkably unconcerned about this, and just told me to throw it on to the back seat which, like his desk, was littered with files from one job or another. I later learned that Mr Rayer always put his case on the car roof as he got into the car, then hooked it down with his stick. Unfortunately he quite often forgot the second part of the exercise and the office frequently got telephone calls with the news: 'Mr Rayer's driven off with his brief-case on the car roof again!'

We arrived at the Nash holding without incident, which in itself was an achievement. The next three days passed much as the first. Dai and his mates were pulling machinery out of the barns and outbuildings like men demented. I'm bound to say that when the chips were down the three of them worked as if their lives depended on it, determined to finish their share of the sale on time. Whether it was in anything like the right order was another matter. During a quick break for a cup of tea I complimented Dai on the way his team were getting along.

'Yer gaffer man's been very good to me, pleased to help 'im out,' he replied, his simple words again demonstrating the loyalty and respect that Mr Rayer commanded.

I wish I could say that I was progressing as efficiently inside the house. Unfortunately Mr Rayer insisted on helping me, which probably explained why Dai was getting on so well outside. We seemed to have lot numbers on everything, but how the public would be able to view it was beyond me. There was furniture, glass, old prints, china and the like everywhere, all jumbled up. When I expressed some concern to my boss, I was told that we would be getting to the farm early on sale day to move the furniture outside so that everyone would be able to view. That ensured that I shouldn't have too late a night in the pub on Friday: we would have to be there at about five o'clock in the morning. By Thursday evening, to my relatively untrained eye, everything appeared to be accounted for according to Mr Rayer's office catalogue, although in terms of order the effect would have been the same had it all just been thrown up in the air and left where it landed.

'Don't worry, Philip, you'll see how it all works. As long as it's got a number on it everyone will know it's for sale.'

Who was I to argue? That, I thought, was that; just a quiet Friday tidying things up. Then I heard the words that struck terror into my heart.

'Philip, you can help Mr Nash and me sort out Hector tomorrow and you'll have to lead him on the sale day.'

Great. What excuse could I give to avoid this impending horror? Feigning illness, developing a sudden allergy to bulls or even suggesting that Dai would be the man for the job? But I couldn't pass the buck. It was all to no avail. I didn't sleep too well that night, waking up periodically in a cold sweat imagining being gored to death by the so-called friendly Hector. The journey to the farm the next morning was very quiet.

'You haven't much to say for yourself, Philip. Hope you haven't had a heavy night;

we've got a tough day ahead of us today.'

The last part of this remark did not help the air of doom that was beginning to descend upon me. We arrived at the farm with a plan to build a sales ring out of old gates and fences so that Hector could be paraded in front of potential bidders. Eventually we lashed up some sort of ring with wooden gates and baler twine. Hector was to be brought down from the fields and kept in one of the stables overnight. Time to make myself scarce.

'Philip, you'd better come with me.'

Off I wandered like the condemned man. At least he got a meal of his choice and a chance to say a few words before his fate was delivered. I was given a piece of rope which had to be passed through a brass ring in Hector's nose. The rope was about four feet long, which meant I wasn't going to be any more than a pace and a half from him at any one time. After my initial nervousness things didn't seem to be going too badly as, without incident, we made it up to the stable near our makeshift sales ring in the farmyard. Perhaps he wasn't so awful after all. Things now weren't looking quite so gloomy. While I couldn't fathom out how the sale would proceed the next day, my employer seemed happy enough with our progress.

I was up with the sparrows on Saturday morning; it was a sunny day but the sky was sprinkled with the odd dark rain cloud. I was excited about my first farm sale, anxious not to let Mr Rayer down, but trying to put all thoughts of Hector out of mind. Having arrived at the farm, the first task was to take as much of the furniture as we could manage outside. We were over an hour into the job when the gathering rain clouds produced a deluge.

'Better get this lot back in the house, Philip. They'll have to view it in there.'

Everything we had spent the last hour and a half moving out of the house now had to be put back. It was in even more of a mess than it had been before we started. Halfway through this task, with Dai in charge of logistics, and pieces of furniture piled one on top of another in the farmhouse, the downpour stopped and the clouds cleared.

'Better get this lot back out again, Philip, it'll be easier to view outside.'

This was getting ridiculous; it was nearly eight o'clock with viewing starting in an hour's time and Dai wasn't sure if he was moving the outside stuff in or the inside stuff out. I looked up at the sky again; it was ominously dark. Sure as eggs is eggs it started to spot with rain; I looked at Dai and he looked at me, both of us trying to avoid eye contact with Mr Rayer, who had been conducting operations like a traffic policeman. He then came out with a remark that

I have never forgotten to this day: 'Drop of rain won't hurt this good furniture, may as well get it all outside.'

The sale was to start at ten o'clock with the furniture, followed by the implements and ending with Hector – just to prolong my agony for as long as possible.

The auction actually got under way at about ten fifteen, which apparently was then a record for Mr Rayer. My job was to clerk for the auctioneer and write down the buyer's name and the price next to the lot number and description on the sale sheets. The sheets were then passed to Hinge and Bracket, seated in a makeshift office, who would enter all the information into a sales ledger. Mr Rayer conducted the auction himself, and while most auctioneers will sell at a pace of about 100 to 150 lots per hour, EEFR restricted himself to a sedate 50 to 60 lots in the same time.

He had an interesting stance when he was selling. In order to rest his one good leg he would balance, a little like a stork, on his tin leg. But on this occasion he had dropped his tin leg on to my foot and was resting his hefty sixteen-and-a-half-stone frame on my toes. I tried to slide my foot from under his leg but he obviously couldn't feel a thing. Every time I tried to ask him to move it he cut me short with, 'Not now, Philip, I'm trying to sell.'

There was nothing else I could do except grin and bear it.

Farm sales tended to be treated as a day out by many, so the atmosphere was very jolly. There were buyers of vintage tractors and implements in abundance, the grape-vine having worked overtime with the news of the disposal of Gilbert Nash's collection – which I had discarded as tat. And among them, some well-known antique dealers. I couldn't see why they were there; obviously something had caught their eye.

'Lot number 127, a silver-plated bowl. Bid me.'

'Fifty pence!' shouted the wife of a local farmer.

'One pound!' shouted another, and on it went, my boss shouting out, 'One fifty, two, two fifty, three, three fifty, four, four fifty,' and so on.

Suddenly one of the dealers shouted, 'Ten pounds!'

Mr Rayer ignored him and up we went in 50 pence bids. And on and on. Another dealer now joined the fray.

'Sixty-seven fifty, sixty-eight, sixty-eight fifty, sixty-nine, sixty-nine fifty, seventy–'

'For God's sake, man, one hundred pounds,' shouted the first dealer.

'Seventy, seventy pounds fifty, seventy-one, seventy-one fifty, seventy-two...'

On we went, through £100, then £200

and finally £300 – all in 50 pence bids. It was taking us an age.

'Three hundred and seventy-one fifty, three hundred and seventy-two, three hundred and seventy-two fifty, three hundred and seventy-three, three hundred and seventy-three fifty, three hundred and seventy-four, three hundred and seventy-four fifty, three hundred and seventy-five.'

Then silence. I wasn't sure if everyone had dropped off to sleep or whether we had finally reached the end. Thankfully it was the latter. Mr Rayer, for some reason best known to himself, tended to stick to the same increment he had started with and never increased this figure no matter to what level the bidding rose. I later discovered the bowl was a rare piece of Scottish silver and made probably what it was worth.

The implements and tractors all made what appeared to me to be a fortune. Even the piles of scrap fetched world record prices; apparently there were rare engine parts mixed up among it all. With none of the outside lots in any order, the auction started to look like a nature ramble as auctioneer, clerk and the assembled crowd wandered from machine to machine trying to find the right lot. I must say they were all very patient – I'm sure they wouldn't have been with anyone else.

At last came the moment I was dreading.

We were standing by Hector's sale ring.

'I'll book for myself, Philip–' (this meant Mr Rayer would record the buyer and the price paid himself) – 'you go and lead him round the ring.'

I climbed in, trying not to show my nerves, although remarks like, 'Look, it's 'im with the soot in the ship pens,' following me didn't help.

I took a firm hold of the rope and tried to keep control of the bull as I led him around the ring. All went well until Hector caught sight of Mr and Mrs Nash out of the corner of his eye. He took off while I hung on grimly to the rope behind him, straight through the makeshift wooden fences and towards his owners. I was beginning to fear for my life, a concern that didn't seem to spread among the gathered crowd, who I could clearly hear laughing. I tried to keep my cool as I was dragged behind Hector, still hanging on to the rope. Eventually we came to a halt by Mrs Nash, who reached into her pocket and produced one of her chews. I could see she was not the only toffee addict as she popped a small handful into Hector's mouth. Hector was now seemingly contented; I was not to know that he always behaved like this when he saw his owner's wife who had obviously given him a sweet tooth. Gilbert looked fondly on and scratched him between the eyes saying, 'Told you he was friendly, young man, wouldn't hurt a flea.'

This had not done my street credibility any good, particularly after the sheep episode. Still, as Mr Rayer said, with perfect seriousness, 'You've got to take control of situations like that, Philip; an auctioneer always has to be in control.'

I couldn't help an inward chuckle, remembering the haphazard way we had lotted up the sale. Still, the Nashes were delighted – and, for all my efforts, I was even given an extra bag of toffee by Mrs Nash.

Lot 4

Algebra and Turkey

The old Triumph never ran well even when it was running well and today it was definitely not running well. I had a certain empathy with it in that I felt decidedly off colour too, whether because of Mr Rayer's driving or just because I was below par, I was unsure.

Mr Rayer had arranged to pick me up from home at about six thirty in the morning. Mr Rayer being Mr Rayer he arrived at seven o'clock but I had no doubt we would make up the time later in the day. The year was

1978 and we were just ten days away from Christmas. We had a busy day ahead of us: I was travelling with him towards Monmouth to help him put the finishing touches to a large farm valuation and then we had to drive back to Bromyard to conduct the firm's annual Christmas auction sale of dressed turkeys and other poultry.

I love frosty December mornings but, unfortunately, this was not one of them. We had experienced almost two solid weeks of torrential rain and, while it appeared to be slowly clearing, the clouds were still dark and steady rain fell. The city of Worcester is divided by the River Severn on a north–south axis and at times like this, with the river in full flood, the traffic comes to a standstill. It is a nightmare to try to navigate through, however well you know the back roads and rat-runs that normally cut valuable minutes off journeys. Now, Mr Rayer did not like driving on motorways, so I had never had the joy of experiencing one with him. It was a pleasure I was very happy to defer. Normally he would have crossed through the centre of the city and travelled to Monmouth by way of the minor roads, but we were on a tight schedule and my heart sank when he announced, 'I think we'll give the M50 a try.'

Our journey to get on to the motorway was uneventful – for Mr Rayer. We only cut up

61

three cars and had horns blown and lights flashed at us four times. Having suffered innumerable nerve-racking trips with the major this was relatively incident-free. Despite a tranquil trip, however, I was feeling really unwell, shivering with cold, with a rasping sore throat. My biggest concern was the Rayer pipe. I knew that once the charred tobacco burner came out of his pocket and was ignited I had the choice of opening the window and further freezing or leaving it shut and having a throat that felt like barbed-wire strands were being pulled down it. It was like offering the condemned man the choice of either the noose or the firing squad. Added to which I had a head that pounded as if it were being used as a test bomb site.

Once on the M50 it started to rain a little harder, nothing like as bad as we had been experiencing, but rain none the less. It was at this point that the old Triumph decided to get its own back for the years of abuse it had suffered. The windscreen wipers did not have an intermittent wipe facility so it decided to create one: very intermittent. They would wipe the screen clear and then stop for no reason at all. When or whether they started again was a matter of luck, with the net result that Mr Rayer could hardly see where we were going. I just sat there thinking of all the things I hadn't done in my life that I was now unlikely to achieve, as catastrophe could only be just around the corner. Mr Rayer squinted through the windscreen in the way that tank commanders peer through the slits in the turret during battle. My boss thankfully cut his speed to about thirty-five miles an hour. My sense of relief was overwhelming, until for some reason he pulled out into the over-taking lane and just stayed there – at a steady thirty-five miles an hour.

'There's less surface water out here, Philip, we should get along better.'

The logic of this escaped me: there were no vehicles in front of us to throw up any spray so I couldn't see why we had pulled out. But I didn't feel able, or well enough, to question my boss's driving. After a while, however, there was a huge tailback of vehicles behind us, all with normally functioning windscreen wipers, all eager to get on with their jour-neys. I sat back in the seat and not for the first, or the last, time tried to pretend that I was not there. By the time we got off the motorway there must have been miles of cars and lorries behind us. Fortunately we could not hear what they were undoubtedly saying about us. We eventually arrived at our destin-ation.

The farm overlooked the River Wye as it meandered its way south, with the house and buildings sitting high on a hill. Our job was to finalise the annual valuation required for

the farmer's trading accounts. In professional terms this was called a live and dead
stock valuation and involved looking not
only at the cattle but also the crops, machinery and the like. Mr Rayer had dealt with the
bulk of the report but, so he told me, needed
my help 'with a few counts'. It was now
raining fairly steadily and Mr Rayer, stick,
clipboard and stubby, inch-long pencil in
hand, walked round to the boot of his car to
put on his waterproofs. He produced what I
can only describe as a piece of tarpaulin that
looked as if it had been used for target
practice. There were holes all over it with a
larger one in the middle that his head went
through. Once he tied it around his waist
with a piece of baler twine, he looked like a
badly loaded lorry. I stood there, watching
the pantomime of Mr Rayer climbing into
his survival kit, and realised that I was slowly
getting wetter, feeling rougher and had no
protection of my own from the elements. At
this point my thoughtful boss pulled out his
number two wet weather sheet and a yellow
souwester for me to wear. I just hoped and
prayed that we wouldn't meet anyone I knew
and that no one had a camera to record our
motley appearance. If we had worn our
underpants on the outside of our trousers
the picture would have been complete: Bat-
man and Robin to the life. Off we marched
to finalise the valuation.

We arrived at an open barn full of hay. My job was easy: count up the bales. Well, it sounded simple enough, and probably was, until Mr Rayer produced an archaic book to help me. I would guess it was written in Edwardian times and, as I looked through the chapters to find the information relevant to my current task, I saw mention of rods, poles, perches and other unfathomable things that people in the real world never used. At last I found the chapter I needed, and at that moment Mr Rayer announced that he was off to look at something he called the turnip clamp. The little book he had lent me was a mine of information but unfortunately the hay bale measuring section required a level of maths in general and algebra in particular that was way beyond my comprehension. I tried to work the wretched thing out and came up with an answer of 585 bales. I knew Mr Rayer would want me to be thorough and so I applied the formula again as a double check. This time my equation came to 423 bales. A third attempt totalled something over 650 bales. The only answer was to get into the middle of the stack and physically count them.

I was now wet through, my borrowed waterproofs being worse than useless, and I was feeling thoroughly miserable; I was beginning to think that the teaching profession was a better option and I had made a terrible decision in quitting the blackboard jungle. My count this time resulted in a total of 736 bales. So much for the academic approach.

I wandered over, with some trepidation, to where I could see the major working. He enquired whether I had got an accurate count of the bales using the magic formula. I nodded a little sheepishly and quickly asked what we should do next.

'We need to count the turnips.'

This filled me with horror as I imagined I would be left on my own and would end up counting the things one at a time. Fortunately I was wrong.

Part of the barn he was looking at had railway sleepers forming a wall in a rectangular shape that enclosed a huge pile of small rugby ball-shaped things that I assumed were the turnips. Mr Rayer was carefully taking various measurements and then produced a slide rule. I had no idea what he was doing and the way I was feeling, I have to admit, I did not really care.

'That little book's a godsend, Philip. You seemed to grasp the principle quicker than most; the turnip formula should be quite easy after that.'

I could see me being asked to work out the circumference of an average turnip and multiply it by some strange formula; it was time to answer an urgent, and timely, call of nature. I told him that I had better pop to find a suitably secluded corner of a barn and strode off before he had a chance to say anything. I wandered out of sight and stood under the shelter of a tractor shed and paused for breath. I was drenched to the skin (not just from the rain as I was now sweating buckets), my head thumped and I was shaking with chills. This felt worse than a normal cold but I didn't dare say a word to a man who suffered constant pain from his disability every day of his life and never uttered a word of complaint.

'Ah, there you are; we've got to go and count the cattle in the river meadows.'

This was turning out to be the maths lesson from hell. What was the formula for counting cattle? Personally I favoured using the fingers on my hands. I knew the cattle were in a field by the river at the bottom of a steeply sloping hill and the thought of walking down there, and more importantly climbing back, was making me shiver even more.

'We'll need to borrow the farm Land-Rover to get down there,' Mr Rayer said.

This was really appealing; for five minutes at least I could sit in the dry with the heater on. As we walked around the corner to where the 'Lanny' was parked my heart sank. I should have guessed this would not be the latest off-roader. It was a 1953 example with a canvas roof. At least, it should have been canvas but it looked more like a lattice of very holey ribbon. A heater was out of the question. I walked towards the driver's door, assuming that I would be doing the driving as these trucks did not have the option of an automatic gearbox.

'Jump in the passenger side, Philip. The slope down there will need some careful driving.'

If I had not been involved perhaps I could have seen the funny side of that remark. There was little point in telling Mr Rayer that the Lanny was manual so I sat in the passenger seat as I was told.

I have always loved old films. I think it was Kenneth More playing Douglas Bader in *Reach for the Sky* who drove an old Bentley and used a walking stick to engage the clutch to change gear. Mr Rayer had climbed into the driver's seat, started the engine and pushed his ever present stick on to the clutch. With the touch of a country blacksmith he grated the gear lever into place. When he planted his good leg on to the accelerator the revs built up to a level far exceeding that recommended in the driver's manual. Suddenly the muddy end of his walking stick slipped off the clutch and we shot forward over the brow of the hill and down towards the river meadow. The incline was very steep, about one in four, I would have said, and we seemed to be going down it at a rate well in excess of any safe speed. I was thinking about how I could tactfully suggest we should slow down a little when Mr Rayer took his good leg off the accelerator and stamped it on the brake. No response. The rain was running in torrents down the slope of the incredibly muddy field and rendered the Land-Rover an unstoppable two-ton sledge. We were hurtling towards the swollen, and fast-moving, waters of the River Wye.

Suddenly my sore throat and headache didn't seem that much of a problem. I was panicking and about to say something when I saw Mr Rayer reach for his pipe and matches. Totally unfazed, he thought it the ideal opportunity for a smoke. I decided to sit back and let fate decide our destiny. As the rain came through the smoke-filled cab I was wondering just how cold the river would be as we slid into it, when we came to a halt ten feet from the water's edge. I sat there shaking, unsure whether the shivering was the result of my cold or a combination of terror and nerves. My boss calmly got out as though this was where he had intended to park all the time and said, 'Philip, you count the bullocks and I'll do the heifers.'

This remark assumed that I knew the difference between the two. I decided that I would count the whole lot, divide the total by two and hope that I was somewhere near to being right. I think I got away with it but to this day I am not sure whether he took what I said or counted the lot himself; I suspect the latter.

In view of our busy day we hadn't stopped for lunch but had worked straight through. We made our way back to the farmhouse where thankfully we were offered tea and cakes. Mr Rayer enjoyed his food and we sat in front of a roaring fire with delightful farmhouse mince pies and tea served on Sunday best china. When Major Rayer called to see his clients he was treated like royalty; and I was lucky enough to share this hospitality. It was the first time I had felt remotely warm during the entire day but was still trembling like a man demented. My headache was almost blinding and the warm tea did little to ease my grating throat. After about twenty minutes my boss made his excuses and we started the journey to Bromyard. As ever he was keen to impart his knowledge to me and we discussed the value of the cattle and turnips as well as the price of hay during the trip. The whole valuation, including all the tractors and implements, came to nearly £800,000. I wondered how much the fee would be for such a large valuation.

'Fifty-four guineas – but we'll include motor hire.' In modern terms that meant to include travelling expenses.

This didn't strike me as being the most profitable of work; I was to discover during my career that the one thing Mr Rayer couldn't value was his time.

The sale of dressed turkeys and poultry only took place once a year, just before Christmas. It was almost like a thank-you party for the locals who had supported the livestock market throughout the year. The venue was the hotel in the middle of the town and all the local farmers' wives brought in their Christmas fare that had been specially fattened up for the occasion. The sale was to take place in the ballroom on the first floor of the hotel and I discovered that my role was to carry all the entries for sale from the ground floor up the stairs to the ballroom, then lot up the sale and finally clerk for Mr Rayer as he sold the lots. I was, if anything, feeling worse and my energy level was at an all-time low. Carrying trays of huge fat turkeys up a flight of stairs was not helping. Mr Rayer, who seemed oblivious to all forms of discomfort, had decided to open every window in the ballroom 'as it would keep the lots fresh'. The wind blew the rain in through the wide-open windows; there seemed no escape for me today. To add to my woes I then had to distinguish between plucked turkeys, chickens, cockerels, ducks and geese. Without feathers they all looked much the same to me. The farmers' wives took great pleasure in pulling the leg of the new boy who couldn't tell what his Christmas lunch looked like. Beads of sweat were running off my brow as I shuddered with cold. Mr Rayer at last began to notice that I was under the weather and said I ought to wrap up warm.

'I'll go and get you a rug, Philip.'

Before I could say no or protest he strode off with that unique straight-leg gait that his artificial limb necessitated. That made me feel incredibly guilty: here was a man who never let his severe disability affect anything in his life that he wanted to do offering to help his young pupil who had a bit of a cold. I felt even worse on his return. He was carrying a multicoloured blanket from one of the hotel bedrooms; quite what I was expected to do with it I did not know. He knew, however, and proceeded to wrap it around me like a poncho from a low-budget Clint Eastwood spaghetti western. I didn't have the heart to tell him that the pain to my dignity was greater than the benefit his blanket gave me. Every time one of the farmers' wives walked past there was a ribald comment.

'You look like a refugee dressed like that. Don't stick the label on the wrong end; that's the parson's nose, young sir,' and, 'Do you know where to stuff it? The blanket not the bird,' were but two.

Few people realise that it's basically the

same amount of work to sell a £10,000 lot as it is a £10 lot. Christmas poultry was hardly likely to break the £10 barrier. The sale was due to start at six o'clock and normally the 200 lots would all have found new owners by eight o'clock. With Mr Rayer selling at his normal rate by eight o'clock we were just about halfway through and there was now a veritable gale blowing through the ballroom. Mr Rayer didn't have a public address system and shouted out the bids within six inches of my ever throbbing head. Most of the buying clientele were also hardy farmers' wives who were used to working in a room where the elements battered the occupants. It struck me as strange that the ladies seemed to bring lots in to sell only then to try to buy the same amount back from the lots that had been brought in by their neighbours.

Lot after lot, the bidding rose by 10 pence at a time. The farmers' wives were a careful, canny lot and the bidding was not too dissimilar to pulling teeth. This sale was taking on the proportions of an epic such as *War and Peace*.

One lady in particular, standing on the other side of my boss, was getting more irate as the sale went on, complaining bitterly that Mr Rayer had refused to take her bids.

'Major Rayer, I've bid on most of the last twenty lots and you've ignored me.'

'I'm sorry, madam, but I haven't seen you

73

lift your hand once.'

'I haven't, Major Rayer, I didn't want me neighbour see the lots I wanted to bid on. I stood here so I could tap you on the leg when I wanted to bid.'

'Well, you'll have to come round and tap on the other one – that one's tin.'

The audience burst into laughter as the lady turned scarlet and shuffled round to the other side.

At ten minutes past ten the sale finished. It had barely realised £1,500. Mr Rayer regarded this sale as a charitable event and, much to the consternation of his colleagues back at the office, reduced his commission rates as a token of the season's spirit. The net result was, roughly, another 54 guineas to match the amount we had earned in the morning.

Although Christmas was coming and the goose was getting fat, the auctioneer most definitely was not. It had been about fifteen hours since we left home this morning and we had earned 108 guineas between us. While I knew my time was worth very little, Mr Rayer clearly was not of the commercial world. Ernest Edward Foley Rayer was not in this business to make money.

Ever generous, Mr Rayer decided to treat myself and some of the farmers who had come to watch the evening's sale to drinks and food at the hotel. His gesture was well received. By my calculations our net profit for the day after entertaining expenses was about 6 guineas.

I went home feeling completely drained, and as rough as a bear's bottom. I went straight to bed and struggled to rise from it the next morning. A trip to the doctor diagnosed glandular fever and I was off work for nearly three weeks. Mr Rayer, generous to a fault, ensured that Lucozade and grapes were never in short supply during my recovery. I should think his regular Red Cross parcels of glucose drink and fruit accounted for the remaining 6 guineas of our day's work.

Lot 5

Potatoes £5 a Bag

In those early days as a trainee finances were always tight but it didn't seem to stop me from having a good time. Most weekends, and some weekday nights, I could be found at the Greyhound, the local pub in the village where my parents lived. I was still living with them which enabled me to eke out the beer money a little longer, but I still don't know how I managed it.

My drinking partner in those days was a

fellow young auctioneer by the name of Jim Johnson, who worked for another local firm called Lloyds and Gold. Jim and I were the same age, loved sport and enjoyed a pint. We were also both up the same financial creek without a paddle, or much hope of finding one. Our financial crisis came to a head after a weekend particularly heavy on the wallet and the liver. We simply had to come up with a scheme to improve our bank balances. We were both at the very early stages in our auctioneering careers and it would be no use asking our employers for a pay rise. As it was we were probably paid more than we were worth. But our salvation was sitting in front of our noses.

Many of the farmers in the village grew produce – indeed my own father was involved in market gardening at the time – and it occurred to Jim and me that if we bought produce from him we could sell it to some of Jim's contacts in the Birmingham area and make our fortune. This was so obviously the way forward, we realised we could teach the other locals a thing or two about the job; after all, most of them were only the second or third generation of farmers. Potatoes were going to be our first purchase. Spuds were the staple diet of the nation – how could we fail? We decided to outline our plan to my father, who gave a wry smile, but humoured his only child by agreeing to sell the new partnership two tons of potatoes in eighty half-hundred-weight sacks at £2 per sack. Not only that but we got credit and free storage as well.

There are times in your life when good luck, or I suppose bad luck, walks up and hits you in the face for no apparent reason. Overnight the price of half-hundredweight sacks of potatoes went from £2 to £5 a bag. I think it was due to a shortage caused by a drought that year. These hard-working local farmers had no doubt seen it all before, but we were suddenly feeling like really cute businessmen. The next step was to sell them. Jim's contacts in Birmingham wanted regular deliveries, and we had to do just that – deliver. This was a minor setback in that we had no means of transport, so it was back to Father to see if we could borrow the farm pick-up truck to carry out our deliveries.

I don't know why, but at this stage I seemed to be cursed with dodgy vehicles. The farm Transit pick-up was right out of the top drawer of dodgy vehicles. Its gearbox had a mind all of its own. The gear lever had an action similar to stirring custard with a stick of rhubarb. The real problem was that the little drawing on the top of the gear knob showing where the gears were supposed to be must have been designed for another vehicle. Not only that, but having located a gear, there was no guarantee that the same gear would be in the same place next time you went to look for it.

As we worked during the week delivery days were always at the weekend. One Saturday afternoon we were driving through Birmingham in the Transit with our last delivery. Thus far the pick-up had behaved in a relatively satisfactory manner. I was following a hesitant learner driver through a fairly busy shopping area. Stop, start, stop – it was a nightmare for the nerves, because the worst thing you could try to do in the Transit was to set off in first gear. Either you stalled because first gear had suddenly become fourth, or, worse still, you clattered into the car behind because reverse had unexpectedly raised its ugly head. The learner had just driven over a zebra crossing and I followed, as the road was clear. Then, for some reason, the learner stopped dead and I had to do the same. Vicious wasn't the right description for the Transit brakes, as Jim found out when his head smacked into the windscreen. Luckily no damage was done to the screen, or his head. The real worry was that hordes of shoppers had chosen this moment to cross the road on the zebra crossing directly behind us, which I had only just cleared. The learner then pulled off in a series of kangaroo lurches that, for once, I would have been keen to emulate.

I tentatively put the gear lever into what I

thought was first and let out the incredibly fierce clutch. Horror. We shot backwards. I sensed what was coming so I already had my hand on the horn. We didn't actually hit anybody but, looking in the mirrors as I hastily located first gear, after three attempts, and drove off, behind us were shopping and bodies everywhere: people trying to get out of my way had knocked one another over. After a quick consultation with Jim, I thought we had better stop and check no one was hurt. I prepared myself for the mother and father of a cussing but strangely the pedestrians' reaction was quite subdued – probably due to shock. So, discretion being the better part of valour, we quickly and quietly slipped off, nervously but without incident.

After selling all the spuds we had made a tidy profit. Thanks to my father's indulgence, we had had no expenses and had more than doubled our money. This game seemed really easy and we couldn't understand why we hadn't thought of it before. Sprouts, we decided, were to be our next venture. The clever part of this new deal was that we bought the sprouts standing, unpicked in a field, and we would pick them ourselves, thereby cutting out all labour costs. This was really going to show the locals how to do it. On the strength of selling two tons of potatoes, we could see ourselves revolutionising the market gardening world.

We might even have to consider giving up auctioneering if the sprouts went as well as the spuds did. We knew the strength of any business lay in planning for the future. Our meetings took place in the Greyhound, which was convenient in every way for us. The field of sprouts that we had bought was in easy walking distance of what had become our corporate headquarters.

Jim and I bought every market gardening magazine going and listened to every produce-related conversation in the pub. One of the snippets we picked up was that sprouts should not be picked until they had experienced a good sharp frost. Even the weather was playing in our favour: the amount of frosts we had had should ensure that our sprouts would be damn nearly unbeatable. We decided we would start picking on Saturday, aiming to finish by lunchtime, then watch a local rugby match in the afternoon. Sprouts in those days were picked in nets of about twenty pounds, I would guess, and it was a very labour-intensive operation.

Saturday morning came and it was bitterly cold. We wore our market wellingtons, jeans, three sweaters each and thick gloves. There were various problems with this outfit. Starting from the bottom, our market wellingtons were of the cheapest variety you could buy. Since you get what you pay for in life, it should have been no surprise to us that they were rubbish: waterproof yes, but they had the thermal warming effect of an ice-cold shower. The three jumpers meant that we moved with all the dexterity of a Michelin man, and the thick gloves rendered us unable to pick the sprouts off the plant that they were frozen to. Ah well – no pain, no gain. Off with two of the sweaters, off with the gloves and ignore the frozen feet. Well, after we had been at this for about three hours frostbite seemed a real possibility. We both thought that once we had gone through the tingly, numb stage, we would be all right. We were wrong. The pain was unbearable. We had picked barely enough sprouts for Sunday lunch for a small family that didn't like the damn things. At about one o'clock we thought we would adjourn to the pub. A revision of tactics was called for. We still had about three acres to pick and our aim of short-term, quick profit was looking a bit unlikely.

As we walked into the Greyhound bar we sensed a few knowing looks from the regulars whom we had regaled with our stories of potato success. What we hadn't realised was that if they stood on the window seats at the end of the pub, they could see our every pitiful move in the sprout field. It cost 75 pence to get a net of sprouts picked that might sell for just under £1 at market. After our success with the potatoes we had, in retrospect rather too generously, promised to pay my father, not only for the cost of the sprout nets, but also for the storage and use of the dodgy Transit. You did not need to be the Chancellor to understand that we were in trouble. To pay for them to be picked, along with these expenses, would have cost far too much. Many of the regulars in the bar offered to buy them back from us, but the embarrassment would have been too great even to consider. There seemed to be only one answer: retreat with tails firmly between legs. This we did, deserting a field full of frozen sprouts, hoping it would not seem too obvious from the window seats in the Greyhound.

The net result was that, financially, we were now back where we had started before the potato deal. It stopped our plans for world fruit and vegetable domination and reinforced one of the old adages that my father had always told me: If you want to find a fool in the country bring him with you. We also had to endure much ribbing from the local farming fraternity, but it was so good-natured that we were bought free beer for about a month afterwards.

Given the theory of the sprouts improving with frost, this should have been a bumper year for them. The frost had barely left the ground for what seemed like weeks. After freezing in the field the offices in Worcester were a warm haven, where the central heating system was turned up to full chat to keep Hinge and Bracket warm. The temperature in the front office seemed to be exaggerated by the fog from the cigarettes the two chain-smoked all day. The Friday after the great sprout extravaganza found me in the office at something of a loose end, making sure that I kept my head down and stayed in the warm, not wishing to venture out into the Arctic-cold weather. I was trying desperately hard to avoid the major, who was always able to find a job for idle souls; indeed, it seemed to me that he found it his duty. A 'Mr Rayer job' was never simple, never took less than about five hours and was to be avoided at all costs on a Friday lunchtime. His total lack of any concept of time was legendary and to be caught now would ruin any chance of an early start to the weekend. The old joke about what goes ninety-nine-bonk (a centipede with a wooden leg) struck terror in all those in the office, except in this case it was one-bonk, the noise the Galloping Major used to make coming down the stairs. Quite why he insisted on having an office on the first floor no one knew; I suppose it was yet another indication of his dogged independence. Suddenly on this particular Friday, just before two o'clock, the dreaded one-bonk signalled the appearance of Mr Rayer. Members of staff instantly locked themselves in lavatories, disappeared into broom cupboards and generally made themselves scarce. This time I was too slow.

'Philip, we're off to doings.'

Bang goes my Friday night in the pub, I thought resignedly, as the sky suddenly became very dark. I didn't have a clue who or where 'doings' was. Like a lamb to the slaughter I followed him out through the back door of the office to where Thunderbird IV was parked. I got in and remembered that the heater was slightly less warming than a spent match. As we set off, for once, I was keen for Mr Rayer to ignite his pipe as I thought it might improve the temperature somewhat.

Burton Hall was a monster of a house; in fact, house probably wasn't the right word – aircraft hangar would have been more appropriate. The Hall had been built at the end of the nineteenth century by a wealthy Birmingham industrialist and was a huge stone pile. The entrance hall was big enough to park three double-decker buses; each tile in the huge black and white floor was more like a paving slab of about three feet square; and most of the wild life in Africa seemed to be hanging from the walls in the hall. There were deer of every kind, lions, tigers, bears and, worst of all, horrible elephant-foot wastepaper bins. The fortunes of the family who lived here, the Slaters, were dwindling, and the coffers had very nearly run dry. This was obvious from the general state of the Hall, which looked like it needed vast sums of money spent on it that they didn't have. That was why we were there. Colonel Slater wanted to sell an estate cottage to help sort out a serious case of dry rot in the cellar.

My God, it was so cold in that house, it was warmer outside than in. We were met by Mrs Slater in an overcoat. She showed us to the library, where Colonel Slater joined us. They were lovely people, aged about seventy and very gentle. As only the two of them lived in the whole place, they used a very small apartment over the kitchen, which was at the far side of this enormous house, but in honour of our visit they had opened up the library, which like the rest of the building was full of lovely antique furniture, paintings and other fine objects, with the added charm of a collection of finely bound books. The four of us huddled around a two-bar electric fire that had a long, considerably frayed flex and sat on a threadbare Turkish carpet. I was the odd one out in that I didn't have an overcoat on, primarily because I didn't possess one. Mrs Slater asked if we wanted tea – coffee in places like this was never an option – and vanished for what seemed like hours. When she reappeared our tea was in Thermos flasks, Mrs Slater explaining that the kitchen was so far away it would have been stone cold with conventional pots. Mr Rayer began to discuss the business and, bearing in mind he was a man incapable of ignoring his own red herrings, I knew we were in for a long old haul. My role in the proceedings was to sit, listen and learn. I was there as the pupil, eagerly waiting to pick up any pearls that might drop my way. Jim Johnson would be in the pub without me this evening.

But to tell the truth, I didn't seem to mind. The whole house captivated me. Wherever I looked I saw wonderful furniture and lovely collectors' pieces. Every corner of the room contained some gem or other. Exhibition-quality nineteenth-century walnut furniture, landscape paintings with just a hint of Constable or Turner, game books recording the bag of enormous family shoots at the turn of the century: a mosaic of social and domestic history from an age gone by. In a way the most appealing feature was not the contents, but that they were situated in their original environment, even if it was now crumbling. In some cases the ravages of time had taken a toll: this was a private museum crammed with items. Yet I was totally entranced. A fuse had been lit inside me and I had a burning desire to handle these wonderful pieces, and find out more about them. Further, to learn about their owners, their history and the homes in which they lived. If I had anything to do with it, my days helping Dickie in the market were going to be numbered. This was the world in which I wanted to make my way forward.

My future had suddenly become crystal clear.

Lot 6

Windy and the Walnut Chest

In the early days with Mr Rayer there seemed to be a sale almost every other Saturday. We would move from one part of the county to another, conducting small auctions on the clients' premises. These were not the grand affairs of the type conducted by the London salerooms when they move en masse to dispose of the contents of large country houses. Ours were at the other end of the scale: farm sales of implements and stock where retirement was imminent; auctions of the contents of small houses to tie up estates, sometimes only realising a few thousand pounds; and almost anything else that fell under the banner of 'goods and chattels'. This was an all-encompassing title that seemed to enable an auctioneer to sell anything that was remotely movable.

Inevitably this meant there was a lot of

travelling to be done. My father had been most obliging to his only son by lending me the family car, an upmarket German model that he had bought second-hand. It was not top of the range but was his pride and joy and he had worked hard to be able to afford it. So here was his son, driving around the county in a swish car that he had saved up for some twenty years to own. Owing to my perilous financial situation, my poor father also had to provide the petrol for its not so economical engine. The sale in two weeks' time was to be at the north-west of the county, the estate of the late Jeremiah Donne, and was to be another smallish sale. After my baptism with the Gilbert Nash sale it was now my job to go and help lot up these auctions, so I had to have some form of transport to get to the sales venues.

My father decided that his last act of indulgence towards his son would be to buy him a car. My imagination ran riot: I felt a sporty little Italian number would be appropriate, definitely in red, and I could just see myself cruising around the city, the envy of all. My father reasoned that as I was now working for a firm of auctioneers we should buy my car from an auction. Cars were sold on Saturdays and on an evening midweek. One such evening we found ourselves looking at the selection of cars on offer. There seemed to me to be more sheepskin coats, suede shoes and acres of plastic filler in rusting wings than I had ever seen before. Not only that, but there didn't seem to be any sporting numbers, Italian or otherwise. So much for my dreams.

My father had resolved that we should go for a sensible English option, and there it was: a mark one Ford Cortina. Not only was it the base-level entry model (no GT suffix with this one) but it was the most lurid shade of pea green. There was no apparent filler either; no one had thought it worth while bodging, judging from the rust in the wings. This was the one my father had decided upon and my spirits had sunk so low that I was in no state to argue. He went on to tell me that, in accordance with good auction practice, he had set a limit that we would not exceed. I was almost praying for someone else to outbid us but I couldn't see anyone else looking remotely interested in it. Within the hour I was the proud owner of the 'Green Pig' for the princely sum of £25. Well, it wasn't much but it was mine.

It seemed to start all right and after I had removed the 'Sold Without Warranty' sticker from the windscreen I set off. The fuel gauge indicated empty, so my father kindly donated a full tank of petrol to set me on my way.

I had gone about a mile when I noticed an overpowering smell of petrol inside the car.

And that wasn't all: the petrol gauge was moving to the 'E' for empty at an alarming rate. I reasoned that there must be an electrical fault and drove on thinking that it was just a little teething problem that we would need to sort. I smoked cigarettes in those days and I lit one as I pondered the trip home. The tank now appeared to be half full, the smell of fumes was getting stronger and I could hear a sloshing noise in the back of the car. We seemed to be using fuel at a rate faster than the *Ark Royal*. I thought I had better pull over and inspect the back seat to try to identify the problem. The Green Pig had disgorged most of the petrol we had filled it up with over the back seat and foot well. The relevance of the 'Sold Without Warranty' sticker became painfully clear. I instinctively flung the cigarette end out through the car window and headed home as quickly as possible before the level of petrol could rise any higher inside the car and any lower on the gauge.

The Pig had to go and after three days it was sold, remarkably, for a £5 profit, at the Saturday car auction. A replacement Mini was bought from a dealer. It cost more money. The price of the Green Pig was a gift from my father and with the profit from its sale I was still short of funds to buy the replacement car. I had to borrow money from my father again, but at least this time my mode of transport was presentable and kept all its fluids in the right place. Another important lesson learned: auction lots bought in haste may give you a long time to reflect on the wisdom of your purchase.

The little Mini seemed a fine car. It took some time for me to get out of the habit of checking the rear seat nervously, though I never smoked in a car again.

I was quite enjoying the drive towards Jeremiah Donne's former home. For some strange reason it was called the Bridge, although it was not by a bridge; in fact there was nothing resembling a bridge anywhere within the vicinity of the house. Jeremiah had been an agricultural engineer of the most inventive sort, and his workshop adjoined the house. Or maybe it was the other way around, because it was a job to tell where one began and the other ended. Jeremiah's house was so sparingly furnished it was positively Spartan; a prison cell would have had more of an air of luxury about it. There was no electricity, but there was a solid fuel stove that burned its way through the mountain of logs piled up outside the front door. Apart from the stove the kitchen had an upturned tea chest which served as a table, but, strangely, no chair. The sitting room/dining room/office/scrap-metal store had an old, antique-looking chest of drawers, with piles of paper covering its top; the adjoining rooms were stacked with more old metal and curious tools that Jeremiah used in his work. On the first floor was a bedroom with a camp-bed, and a rope suspended across the room on which some of his old clothes still hung. The bathroom was something else. There was an old WC with a green bowl and a pink cistern and a home-made shower that looked like a garden hose. The bath itself, an old enamel example, was full of a gunky solution, and sticking out of it were numerous old bits of metal. Apparently it was his degreasing unit.

His job, I discovered, was to fix the odd and old machines that the locals used on their farms, machines that would all have been beyond economic repair were it not for the inventive skills of the late Mr Donne. It seemed to me that the entire contents of the sale would be made up of piles of junk.

I had a new colleague to help set up this sale, William 'Windy' Brown. William was about five feet six inches tall and barely weighed ten stone. His hair, I later discovered, was silvery white and receding but it was rarely seen because of the smart trilby permanently glued to his head. His nose almost met his chin and the one tooth in his mouth was apparently welded to a huge pipe that would need a team of skilful surgeons to remove. Whenever setting up a sale William always wore a long white smock coat with a broad leather belt around the middle, which was odd enough but paled into insignificance compared to William's most notable, and least desirable, trait. Poor William had a flatulence problem, hence the nickname. Windy William was like an old carthorse with the worst sort of wind; he couldn't take a pace without emitting a rumble. In fact when he occasionally 'missed a beat' it left those in his company wondering if there was something wrong and waiting for him to take the next pace to see that normality returned – which it always did, almost to their relief. I don't think he ever realised why he was always referred to as Windy.

I didn't dare venture down into the cellar that led from the kitchen. It was dark and I was sure would be the home of some unsavoury rodents. Fortunately, having brought Windy along with me, I eventually persuaded him that he should go and have a look down there which, like a good fellow, he did. Shouting from the murky depths below, he let me know that its contents consisted of Jeremiah Donne's only known hobby – home-made wine making. I was later to find out that, apart from being a dab hand at conjuring up odd bits for old machines, he made a damson wine that would fuel the space shuttle.

We spent the rest of the first day trying to sort out what was what. Mr Rayer had told me that sales like this normally started with 'Lot 1: a quantity of scrap' and then moved on with each lot better than the last, leaving the best lot until the end. I thought we might be struggling to improve on Lot 1. Windy was busy sorting out all the bits and bobs into various piles, every step and movement accompanied by his unmistakable trademark. After a while our boss appeared. We knew he'd arrived when he drove the Triumph into the stone steps that led to the front door of the house. He was on his way to another appointment, for which he was about an hour late, but still wandered around the property, often tripping over the piles of scrap on the floor as he lit his fumigating pipe.

'That old chest looks like it might be quite a good thing; I should make that the last lot,' shouted my boss as he left the house, falling down the steps and against his car. Windy and I watched as he hauled himself back up, both knowing that it was useless to offer to help him. His tin leg must have had nearly as many dents as his car.

Windy and I carried on with our task in the house. I decided that I would clear out the old chest, which was covered in all Jeremiah's old accounts and invoices. There was a huge stack of papers skewered on a piece of metal wire sticking up out of a wooden base. This seemed to be his sole filing system, and no doubt it worked for him, but, as far as I could judge, there were some twenty years of bills and accounts randomly spiked on the metal spear. Once I had cleared the top of the chest I could see that below the top a slide pulled out, doubling its size, which rested on two lopers, thin pieces of wood that came out either side of the top drawer. The chest was only about three feet wide and it was fitted with four drawers. The drawers were graduated in size, the deepest one at the bottom, the whole chest standing on small bracket feet. I wasn't sure of its age, the timber it was made of or, more import-antly, its value. It looked really old and the timber, which was a bit tatty, was the colour of chewed toffee – a deep nut brown. I thought I had better ask Mr Rayer to have a closer look on his next visit so that he could give an opinion. He did.

'Walnut, I think, Philip,' was his con-sidered judgement. 'Eighteenth century. They call them bachelor's chests with that type of top – should be a good demand for it.' (I now know that it was actually a chest with a brushing slide as opposed to a bachelor's chest which has a foldover top, rather like a games table.)

I couldn't see it selling well among all the other rubbish at the Bridge but I was sure that Mr Rayer knew what he was talking about. He still hadn't mentioned value but I supposed he knew its worth.

Windy and I continued to sort through all the detritus that was to be sold and eventually we were ready to lot up the sale. Windy's role was to stick on the lot number and shout out a description; mine was to write it all down on the sale sheets. My ability to scribble faster than Windy was the main reason for this. In retrospect it would have been better if Windy hadn't had to move quite so much; the result was like constant rumbling thunder.

'Lot 1: quantity of scrap.'

We piled all the first lot together and made sure that it was easily identifiable before moving on to the next.

'Lot 2: ditto.'

The same process followed. We seemed to be getting on really well and quite speedily.

'Lot 3: ditto.'

Well, this wasn't taxing my literary skills too much.

'Lot 4: ditto.'

This was now getting rather repetitive.

'Lot 5: ditto.'

And on it went until we had lotted up the first 122 lots in exactly the same manner, and only the contents of the cellar and the chest of drawers were left to do. Windy and I looked at one another – this was going to be a most unusual sale. I thought I had better call into the office on the way home and inform Mr Rayer exactly what the fruits of our labour had produced. I was also a little concerned as to whether buyers for the little chest would turn up on the sale day.

'It is what it is and it will make what it will make,' was my boss's observation, which struck me as being philosophical in the extreme for him. He did however agree that he should take the precaution of placing an advert in the antiques trade paper for the little chest. Unusually that was all that was in the advert: one chest; there was nothing else to advertise, certainly not for the antique dealer. The local papers would take care of the other 123 lots.

Mr Rayer felt someone should sleep over at the Bridge on the evening prior to the sale for security reasons. I thought there was more danger of extra stuff being dumped there rather than any of it being stolen, but was eternally grateful when Windy offered to spend the night there.

I arrived at eight o'clock in the morning to find the front door open and no sign of Windy anywhere. I wandered in and called but could see nothing and, more surprisingly for Windy, could hear nothing either. At once I began to get a little nervous, my vivid imagination conjuring up dreadful scenes. In films such scenes always happen in the cellar and that was where I decided to look next. As I opened the door I could hear

Windy groaning; almost reassuringly from both ends.

'Bloody hell, Phil, that's a drop of good stuff. My head feels like someone's put it through a mangle.'

'I'm sorry?' I replied, rather startled.

It then became clear that Windy had been sampling Jeremiah's home brew. Judging by the volume of half-empty, dusty bottles scattered around he had made some serious inroads into every vintage Jeremiah had produced. He was a braver man than I but was paying the penalty now. As I helped him struggle up the wooden cellar steps, they and Windy creaked and groaned in unison.

After I'd poured the contents of my coffee flask into him, Windy began to look like he was going to survive his ordeal, although I wasn't sure for how long. Eventually he staggered to his feet.

We had a queue of some fifty people waiting to view. Of these, about five seemed to be interested in the piles of scrap and the remainder were all over the chest like a rash, turning it upside down, pulling out every drawer and generally going through it with a fine-tooth comb. Windy was pacing around the Bridge like a caged tiger, every step accompanied by a popping noise, like someone stepping on bubble wrap. He said this was in case any troublemaker should tamper with any of the lots of scrap that he had carefully created and labelled. The reality, I suspected, was that he had to keep moving to try to walk off his monumental hangover. I was just happy to stand by the little chest of drawers and pick up all the snippets I could overhear from the dealers. Apparently the general view was that the piece was from the Queen Anne period, about 1705, and was made of a lovely mellowed walnut. This, to a lot of dealers' eyes, was one of the golden ages of English furniture making. The one clue that I was not given concerned its value; all would be revealed at the auction.

Mr Rayer began the auction with me at his side about twenty minutes after it was due to start. This was pretty prompt for him. One of the five dealers who had perused the scrap during the viewing paid £24 for the first lot of scrap. This set the tone for the next 121 lots which all sold for between £10 and £36. Lot 123 I had taken it upon myself to withdraw, having seen the damage it had inflicted on Windy. Then it was the turn of the chest.

'Lot 124: where will you bid me?'

The customary silence then followed; none of the dealers wanted to show their hands too soon. Everyone seemed to be staring at the floor. Eventually one dealer mumbled, 'Fifty pounds, sir.'

Off we went. I had no idea whether this was realistic or optimistic. The bidding just carried on and on. On through £100 and then £500. When we got to £1,000 Windy, for the first and only time I have ever known, suffered his affliction without moving a pace. It even, albeit momentarily, slowed down the bidding.

Finally the hammer fell for the sum of £4,400. As the whole sale only came to £6,786, this was one of the most one-sided sales I have ever been involved with.

I didn't know that much about the business in those days so I wasn't sure if it could have realised more had it been offered in a specialist antique sale and illustrated in a glossy catalogue. However the general view among the dealers I spoke to after the sale was that it had 'made all its money'. This is an expression in the trade that never ceases to be music to the ears of the auctioneer. It proves that the antique bush telegraph normally works well for the auctioneer as the dealers clamour to buy fresh-to-the-market, good quality lots. I am bound to say that in this instance our 'advertising campaign' seemed to have worked more by accident than design.

Lot 7

The £400 Chair

'M'name's Jarn Dee Hoppenheim the third 'n' I'm an Murican anteek deala. I'm over here on a buyin' trip.'

Well, he didn't have to tell me he was an American; while he lacked the traditional ten-gallon hat, everything else about Jarn shouted out the country of his birth. He wore a baseball cap, a New York Yankees T-shirt, tight jeans – in fact overly tight jeans, which perhaps suggested a tendency towards an overindulgence in American burgers, waffles and maple syrup – and a pair of cowboy boots.

'Is Jarn of Danish origin?' I enquired.

'Nope, short for Jarnathen.'

Well, there's English English and American English.

It was about 1980 and I was in the saleroom getting ready for the viewing of one of the firm's auction sales. In those days the sales were not divided into fine art and general: everything that came through the door was entered into the next available sale; you might well have found a Georgian lowboy next to a three-piece suite with an old fridge on the other side. The general viewing was the following day with the sale the day after that. The large and friendly American had asked if he could have a look round early as he was passing through the area. I had been in the job for some four years now and was responsible for the general day-to-day running of the saleroom. Nowadays, with wide use of the Internet, buyers come from all over the world, if not literally then through the phone lines. Most auctioneers put their catalogues on the World Wide Web, which results in enquiries from all over the globe. Twenty-five years ago buyers from across the water were not quite so commonplace. Local dealers sold antiques to other dealers who sold them on again in their turn, with the items eventually finding their way to the shippers who then arranged to export them. The whole process worked its way down a long chain. It was the first time I had encountered an end user from across the pond.

We were standing over an armchair that had been entered by a local lady, Mrs Stratton, who had moved into a nursing home because of heart problems. The firm's partners had rewarded my interest and enthusiasm by letting me loose on the general public: I was now allowed to go out on my own to a few initial inspection visits. The purpose of these calls was to let the clients know what a particular item might make at auction so that they could then decide whether to sell or not. I was really excited and wanted to show my employers that I had the ability to do the job. Preparation was the key, I thought, and I knew that Mrs Stratton had a chair to sell. I spent the evening before my visit reading every relevant article I could find in the few antique magazines that were available in the office and avidly scoured the various price guidebooks I had also taken home. I was confident that Mrs Stratton's chair would hold no mysteries for me. I wore my best sheep market suit, polished shoes and white shirt with my old college tie. I was sure I would impress her with my professional appearance. The appointment was for eleven o'clock and was only ten minutes from the saleroom but I left at ten to make sure that I wasn't late. It always amazed me that old people with various ailments, poor hearts among them, came to Malvern to retire, the whole town being on the side of one of the steepest range of hills in the Midlands. However, all that uphill walking must be beneficial to ill health in general and dodgy hearts in particular; they all seemed to thrive on it.

I arrived at the huge house just outside the centre of town which was now divided into small apartments for the elderly and pressed the bell with Mrs Stratton's name on it. I was greeted by a small, well-spoken lady who showed me to her room. She explained that she had to dispose of the chair simply because she didn't have space for it. I could see what she meant: her small room was packed from floor to ceiling with treasured possessions. There were lovely items everywhere you looked and I was pleased to be able to recognise most of them and, even more importantly, felt confident enough to put a price on them. My research the previous evening into the chair proved the old adage, 'Time spent in reconnaissance is never wasted.'

As I looked around the room my eyes eventually fell on two chairs. Both were armchairs in the sense that they were rather like dining chairs with arms and looked as if they would have originally sat at the end of the dining table. The first was of a type we had sold many times in the saleroom: an early Victorian mahogany version that would make between £200 and £400. The second was completely alien to me; I had seen nothing like it before and it certainly wasn't illustrated in any of the articles I had looked at. I felt the beginnings of a cold sweat and hoped it was the first chair that Mrs Stratton had called me out to look at. I stared at the second chair and frantically tried to think what on earth it might be worth, at the same time willing her to ask me about the first chair instead. Murphy's Law prevailed and Mrs Stratton pointed to the second as I asked her which one she wanted to sell. I gulped and said I felt it might make between £400 and £600. Quite where this figure came from I am unsure, but I reasoned it was better than the first and therefore should make a bit more.

An American dealer had now looked at the chair; I was delighted with the interest shown by the first person to view it and felt a little more confident.

'How much due reckon that preddy liddle chear ull make? Not really the kinda thing I buy but I'd like it fer m'self back home,' the new and potentially important customer asked.

Before I had a chance to answer Jarn said, 'I'd like to leave yer a bid.'

He was unable to attend the sale and wanted to leave a commission bid. This meant that the auctioneer would bid on his behalf at the auction. I was so pleased: Mrs Stratton's chair was very important to me. I hadn't even had the chance to tell Jarn my estimate.

'I'll leave you two forty sterling – make sure you don't run me.'

That wasn't so good. I hesitantly told Jarn of my estimate, hoping he would revise his bid of £240 upwards. He didn't. My smug feeling of self-confidence evaporated. While Jarn said that the chair was not his particular field, his experience was no doubt more likely to prove him right rather than me, given my limited time in the business. My estimate was plainly way over the correct value; my other concern was that if I overvalued items that did not sell I wouldn't be allowed to go out on future appointments. Jarn's remark about not running him indicated a suspicion held by many dealers. Simply that if you leave a bid with an auctioneer he will make sure that it costs the maximum amount you leave by taking bids off the wall to ensure that the top price is achieved. This means creating bids that do not exist. Certainly it has happened and may continue to do so, but it is a practice that I think is wrong as well as unethical. An auctioneer should only use such means when he is trying to reach a reserve figure; this is the minimum selling amount set by the vendor with the auctioneer. In the case of Mrs Stratton's chair the reserve was the lower estimate, namely £400.

I went home that night feeling a little bit low as the first dealer to view the mystery chair had left a bid only slightly more than half the figure I had told Mrs Stratton to expect.

Viewing started officially at ten thirty the next morning and there was the usual clamouring of dealers outside the door at ten fifteen, not so much trying to steal the march on their colleagues in the trade, but simply trying to fit in as many sale viewings in a day as possible. They were, by and large, the local dealers, who attended every sale. Normally they were able to view a sale in less than fifteen minutes, looking for items in their own specialist field, be that furniture, paintings, porcelain, silver or the multitude of items that formed the smalls section. Today was no exception, although my chair seemed to attract more interest than almost all the other lots in the sale put together. Perhaps Jarn was wrong. My spirits began to lift a little.

I wandered up to one of them and asked him what he thought of my chair. This particular dealer attended all my sales and was a good client in the sense that he bid for what he wanted, he paid for his lots and he collected his purchases – what more could an auctioneer want? The buyer who never picks up his purchases, or, worse still, has to be chased for the money is not to be encouraged.

'What's the estimate?'

I hesitatingly told him my thoughts as to what the chair might make.

'I think you're off the mark a bit there, Philip.'

I was beginning to feel quite despondent

that I had overvalued the chair and would have some explaining to do to an unhappy client as well as my employers. Perhaps some unsuspecting soul without the knowledge of Jarn or my other dealer friend would make the same mistake as I had and it still might sell. What baffled me, though, was if I had got it so wrong why was every dealer in the saleroom taking so much interest in it?

The sale had been on view now for about an hour when another of my regular dealers came into the office.

'Philip, what's the chair going to make?'

'Four to six hundred,' I whispered and nervously waited for his reaction; perhaps he could see its potential and would give me some hope that it might just make the reserve. Even if he left me something over £350 I could possibly still sell it and adjust our commission to make sure that Mrs Stratton would not lose out. I might get out of trouble after all.

'Do you want a cheque now?' Goodness, that remark made me sit up. Would I be redeemed and let out again on the unsuspecting public? Perhaps I was right and he would leave a figure between my £400 and £600 estimate.

'Look, I can't make the sale but I'd like to leave you two thousand pounds on it.' That fairly took the wind out of my sails. I was staggered; waves of relief swept over me. The chair would now definitely find a new home, even though I still didn't know anything about it. This was followed up with the statutory, 'But don't run me.'

A sleeper in an auction sale is a lot that is miscatalogued by the auctioneer and accordingly underestimated. Specialist dealers have specialist knowledge, which I have always admired and respected; a general practice auctioneer can never hope to match the in-depth understanding some of these chaps have of a particular subject. My lack of experience looked like making Mrs Stratton's little chair into a bit of a sleeper. The question now was what it would make. I truthfully didn't know – I just hoped that enough dealers would come to the sale tomorrow to ensure that it would sell well.

As time passed more and more fresh faces came into the saleroom and all headed straight for the chair. The antique trade jungle drums had obviously been beating long, loud and hard. Out came the padded seat, it was turned upside down, on its side and every other way possible by all the potential buyers, satisfying themselves before making up their own mind as to its value. There was now a circle of dealers almost three deep around Jarn's 'liddle chear'. Normally dealers are quite canny in the way they view a sale, not letting on to others their interest. In this case the chair must have been so obvious to everyone except me. My nerve endings were beginning to fray with the uncertainty of it all. Perhaps more accurately, it was my uncertainty that caused them to fray. The auction tomorrow was beginning to take on the appearance of a one-lot sale.

The only two bids that had been left by the dealers were Jarn's £240 and the other of £2,000. Not only that, but no phone bids were booked. Normally dealers who were unable to attend the sale in person would book a telephone bid, so they could bid live on the telephone at the auction. Did the fact that no one had done so mean that no one else was interested or would they all attend? I was becoming a nervous wreck. I knew from the bids I had been left and the interest that had been generated that my reserve was hopelessly wrong, but the way things stood at the moment it would sell bang on the reserve figure of £400. There were no other bids to compete against the £2,000 left by the second dealer. The end of the view day came and it was time to go home; I was completely exhausted worrying whether it would make its money – whatever that was.

I arrived at the saleroom early the next morning to find yet more dealers, many of them new faces, eager to view the sale. Among them, the usual collection of local privates – the term used in salerooms for non-dealers – who turned up to every sale come hell or high water. They would bring along their Thermos flasks and sandwiches and sit through the whole proceedings, some rarely bidding on any of the lots on offer. I can see that they came to absorb the atmosphere and excitement of auctions; it was a free day's entertainment in a room rich with characters and drama.

One of these was Mrs Edwards. Whatever the weather she wore an overcoat resembling uncut moquette, the type of material used to cover fashionable three-piece suites of the 1960s. She was always accompanied by her knitting, what seemed like a week's supply of sandwiches and a flask of Bovril. The sofas and sets of chairs to be sold were always at the front of the room, just below the auctioneer, and it was on these that the privates used to sit. Mrs Edwards was normally first in the queue to reserve her seat for the day. She was a large lady, a very large lady, often occupying a sofa to herself. I don't ever remember her buying a single lot, indeed I don't think she even bid on one. She did, however, record every price that every lot sold for in an old school exercise book.

I went into the office to check all was in order for the day's sale and after a few minutes heard a commotion in the saleroom itself. On my return I was scarcely surprised to find the little chair was the focus of attention; there was the usual crowd around the dreaded thing. This time, however, they all seemed a lot more animated. Mrs Edwards had decided this was her chair for the day and it appeared that she had initially been reluctant to leave it so the dealers could inspect it fully. It was now also apparent that having agreed to shift herself, she couldn't; she had welded herself into the chair and couldn't get out of it. The dealers were trying hard to pull her free; their efforts were not doing too much for her dignity, as she was vociferously pointing out. Those elegant cabriole legs – on the chair not Mrs Edwards – were under immense pressure and my saleroom sleeper was in grave danger of being reduced to matchwood as the dealers tried to prise her out. Eventually she shot out like a bar of soap slipping from your hands, muttering that chairs were meant to be sat upon and that she couldn't see what all the fuss was about.

The furniture was to be sold first so I wouldn't have to wait long to find out the secrets of the chair. The auction was conducted by one of Mr Rayer's partners who moved along at a brisk pace without any dramas until we arrived at the chair. He asked for £500; everyone in the room seemed to have their hands glued firmly in their pockets, their eyes staring at their feet; the silence was almost deafening. I couldn't take much more of this. No one wanted to show their hand – literally at an auction – too soon. Eventually a voice shouted, 'Four hundred pounds, sir.'

Well, after I had been left the bid of £2,000 I knew it would sell. It was just a question of whether it would sell for up to the £2,000 that the dealer had left or make more. I need not have worried. On it went in fifties, then hundreds, through the £2,000 figure, then five hundreds and we reached £6,000. It didn't stop there, with three dealers eagerly competing against one another. Then £10,000 and finally at £13,000 the bidding stopped.

'Going once, twice, for the third and last time, any more? Sold: buyer number 27.'

The whole episode had taken only a few minutes. I was very conscious that £13,000 was a long way off the £400 I had told Mrs Stratton. I had instantly stopped being worried as to whether it would sell or not and became highly embarrassed at getting it so spectacularly wrong. Not only that, but I still didn't know what it was. I thought it was a huge sum of money for a single chair. After that the sale seemed a complete anticlimax as all the unsuccessful dealers who had come especially for the chair simply left the room. For them it really was a one-lot sale. The buyer made his way to the office to pay for one of the most expensive pieces I had seen sell at that time. I was keen to find out why it had been so valuable so I summoned up the courage to ask him.

'A Georgian mahogany armchair, Philip – about 1760. Rare and of the best quality. Don't worry, it cost all the money.' Then, a little tongue in cheek, he added, 'Just proves you auctioneers only have to put a lot number on something and let us dealers value it for you at the auction!'

He was right and I was lucky; it had sold well.

An hour after the sale had finished there was a telephone call from Jarn Dee Hoppenheim the third. 'Did I git the chear?'

I replied in the negative.

'How muched he make?' The response brought a whistle down the phone followed by, 'Gee, when it comes to value you were closer 'n me.'

It was a good-hearted remark but didn't help dampen my embarrassment.

There remained one task. I felt I could hardly send a cheque for over £12,000 to a lady with a suspect heart whom I had told to expect £400. I decided to take it round to her personally. I was dreading the call as my embarrassment at being so far wrong with my initial estimate had risen yet further because I fully realised after the sale how little I knew. Mrs Stratton had every right to question me over my opinion of value but I have to say she was really kind and didn't put me on the spot at all; she simply said, 'I knew it was a good chair and thought you were being a little pessimistic. Do you know, we originally had the whole suite. I don't know where they all went to; distributed among the family I suppose.'

My jaw dropped; what on earth would that lot have been worth – and, more to the point, what would I have told her? I shuddered to think.

The partners were delighted with the fee they had earned from the sale of the chair. My embarrassment deepened as it had been my job to value the lots and they relied upon my view. If anything, they made things worse for me by deciding that I would get a small bonus. Twenty pounds was not a fortune but it didn't take me long to decide how to spend it: a first-class reference book on the history of the English chair.

Lot 8

Men in Suits

When I joined the firm I knew that it dealt
with all aspects of general practice estate
agency and auctioneering. It sold terraced
houses and grand country properties; it had
livestock markets and auctioned antiques
and fine art, and dealt with commercial property as well as farms and land. It was an excellent place to learn where the partners and
staff were committed and eager to pass on
tips and knowledge to the newest employee.
What struck me most about the business,
whether with my firm or its competitors, was
the enthusiasm shown by all.

During the early part of the 1980s the
company started to become involved with
insolvency sales. Here assets of a company
that had been put into liquidation, or an
individual who had been declared bankrupt,
were sold off for the benefit of the creditors.

It was on one of these occasions that I
found myself in a warehouse on the outskirts
of a small market town. I had been sent there
to lot up the contents for sale by auction.
The company that had been placed into

liquidation had been in existence for about three generations and made office furniture in general and more particularly office chairs. There were machines there that looked as if they had been made by someone who hadn't got a complete set of plans and had to guess how the last bits fitted together. But the most extraordinary thing was the stock of office chairs that the company used to make. There was a veritable mountain of them, some of them complete and some of them in kit form. There looked, to my untrained eye, as if there was six months' work to get everything ready for an auction sale.

I spent the first day there wandering around and achieving nothing. I could not comprehend the vastness of the job, no matter how many times and from which angle I stared at piles of legs, bases, pedestals and backs as well as the huge quantity of complete chairs. I simply did not know where to start and come four o'clock in the afternoon I decided to head back to the office and see if I could enlist some help. The partner dealing with this particular job was one J. Clifford Atkins. He was the senior partner in the Worcester office and I had met him briefly on my first day when I was placed under Mr Rayer's care.

Cliff had worked in Canada as a commercial real estate agent and, by all accounts, had made an awful lot of money. He was about five feet six inches tall and was always impeccably dressed. His sports jackets, in contrast to Mr Rayer's, were perfectly tailored and always of a flamboyant check. He too smoked a pipe but was a great deal more careful than his colleague and showed no signs of self-inflicted arson attacks. The contrast with his colleague did not end there: while Mr Rayer drove the dreaded Triumph, Cliff had a penchant for extravagant sports cars. There were three other distinguishing traits to J. Clifford Atkins. He had a huge handlebar moustache which seemed to grow ever more luxuriant whenever he was excited, which of course did not affect his skill as an auctioneer, but he was also quite deaf, which was not ideal for a man with a gavel trying to extract the last bid from his audience. His hearing had been affected by gunfire when he was in the army and although he coped with it remarkably well, it did produce some interesting moments. His third characteristic was an expression. Almost every sentence included a 'Right, right', which was normally coupled with 'Jolly good'.

These words were always accompanied by a huge belly laugh that shook his frame and turned his face various shades of red and blue. He would have been a natural as Falstaff or some Dickensian character. His stock phrase rarely contained only one 'right'; sometimes it got as far as 'Right, right, right, right, right – jolly good.'

I told him that I was overwhelmed by the task I had been given and was worried that I would not be able to get everything ready for the sale in three weeks' time.

'Right, right, jolly good.'

I couldn't see what was either right or jolly good about the situation but said nothing; he was the boss and mine was not to reason why. I made the point again, saying that I thought I really did need some help. I wasn't exactly sure that he had heard me as he had bent his head back down over his paper-work, but figured that it was time to leave his office since he was clearly not going to say anything more helpful. When I shut the door behind me he roared, 'You worry too much. Right, right, right.'

I was uncertain whether this was good news or bad but decided to make my way directly to the warehouse the next day and really get stuck into the job in hand. It transpired my boss had, thankfully, heard my pleas: there waiting for me at the door were Dai and Windy Williams. To look at this dynamic duo would not inspire any sort of confidence and yet they always managed to get the job done. Dai spent the day talk-ing to himself, and anyone else who would listen, while Windy spent his time doing what Windy did best. Dai seemed oblivious to the socially suspect behaviour of his workmate but they worked well as a team: Windy issued instructions and Dai ignored them. Lord knows how the combination worked but it did. Things gradually began to take shape as the pair of them sorted out all the office furniture into rows.

This left me to deal with the machinery. The other two decided that this should be my task on the grounds that I had been to college and would know what the machines did. Quite how a qualification in physical education would help with this lot I had no idea; probably the pair of them reckoned it was better to let me loose where I could do the least amount of damage and cause the least amount of chaos. The machines looked as if they had been purchased by the original founder of the company; the newest had to be at least twenty years old. I tried to move some of them around the factory floor but they seemed to weigh several hundredweight each. As an ex-physical education student I used to pride myself on my strength but these were beyond me. All factory shop floors share a certain character, typified by the calibre of the pictures that have been cut out from page three of the *Sun* and, in some cases, from what can only be described as top-shelf magazines. The pin-ups around the walls in this factory were probably cut out and put up the day the machines were installed. I couldn't help but look at these very dated poses and I quietly chuckled to myself at the thought that most of these glamorous girls would now be, at best, well into their sixties and possibly entering their seventies. That is if they were still alive.

I called into the office each night to report to Mr Atkins how we had progressed.

'Right, right, jolly good. Right, right, right.'

The sale was beginning to take shape but my worry now was who on earth would want to buy the acres of office chairs that were assembled in the warehouse; and in some cases were not assembled but consisted of a heap of spare parts. I ventured to suggest that we might well struggle to find buyers for what seemed to be enough chairs to supply every office in the county several times over.

'You worry too much, right, right, right!'

I should have expected this reply by now; an eruption of laughter of volcanic proportions followed. It was time to light his pipe so I left his office through a mist of tobacco smoke. I walked into the front office where Hinge and Bracket were working away, lemon tea to one side of their typewriters and a cigarette in an ashtray to the other. At that point Mr Rayer walked in lighting *his* pipe, sparks flying everywhere. His particular pungent tobacco – which many people swore blind was made up partly of cattle manure – redoubled the smoggy pea-soup atmosphere. This was before the days of non-smoking offices; kippers could have been produced in this one.

It was now time to lot up the sale and after my efforts at Jeremiah Donne's sale I wanted to produce a more descriptive catalogue. That was fine in theory but the practice was a little more difficult. Once you have described one lot of six office chairs, the next identical lot and the ones thereafter really can be nothing other than 'dittos'. The only thing that altered in each lot was the quantity: some times there were six, sometimes ten and sometimes twenty. I had been told that we should sell the 50 lots of plant and machinery first, followed by the 150 lots of chairs, spare parts and other bits and bobs that I couldn't put into any category. Who on earth was going to buy my chair mountain?

I took the catalogue back to the office to be typed up by Hinge and Bracket. This was before the days of word processors, yet the two office ladies churned out catalogues just like shelling peas. They also placed all the adverts and sourced all the specialist papers and journals that would attract the buyers. Vendors are obviously important to auctioneers but the importance of the buyer should not be underestimated, nor – as many forget

– the underbidder, without whom prices would not rise quite as much as we hope. Dealers probably buy the bulk of the items sold at auction, and while they make their living from these purchases, in my eyes their significance cannot be overstated. In this particular instance it was dealers in office chairs and archaic office-chair-making machines that I needed, and needed badly. The thought of no one turning up to the sale was beginning to become a recurrent nightmare.

'You worry too much, right, right, right.' I was getting positively used to this phrase. 'The government surplus boys will be there.'

My puzzled look elicited a further explanation which baffled me even more.

'They do the ministry sales.'

I was now at a complete loss but as the pipe had come out I realised it was time to leave his office. Hinge and Bracket lightened my darkness by telling me that there were sales throughout the country where surplus government stock was sold off by auction. This could be anything from office furniture to Land-Rovers and clothes, the latter normally being under the direction of the Ministry of Defence, hence the term ministry sales. I was in later years to discover that these dealers would buy anything and in huge quantities. I felt a little more relieved to hear this but was still not 100 per cent convinced.

I just crossed everything I had and hoped they would all turn up on the sale day.

And indeed, on the day of the auction, the government surplus boys arrived in droves. Apparently these characters always appear out of the woodwork for sales like this and their accents indicated that they had travelled from all over the country. Most of them drove up in smart cars, for these were not the type of sales where you could pop your purchases into the back of a Volvo estate. More likely a lorry would follow the next day to cart back to base the vast quantities that had been bought; there was little point in these dealers travelling across the country to buy the odd lot. There were, of course, the exceptions to this rule and a few dealers at the lower end of the scale materialised in various vans and pick-ups.

One decidedly odd couple showed up in a very rusty Transit pick-up. He was about fifty-five and dressed in a shiny blue suit with a green check shirt – I could at last see why the expression 'blue and green should never be seen' came about – and black plastic shoes. He might have looked strange in the outside world but in the ministry sales arena he was almost normal; it was his travelling companion who stood out. I guessed that she was his daughter. About thirtyish, she was built like a brick outhouse and wore a bright floral frock like Ma Larkin in *The*

Darling Buds of May, with a filthy, holey cardigan on top. She wore thick milk-bottle-lens glasses, but what really caught the eye was her footwear: sheepskin-lined carpet slippers. The pair wandered around the warehouse with her always a pace and a half behind him. He made copious notes in an old note book with a Ladbroke's pencil and exchanged greetings with the other dealers. She said nothing to them and they said nothing to her. Part of the fun of the job was trying to fathom out who would buy what: what these two would bid on I had no idea.

The sale duly started with the machinery. While I was now confident that the government surplus boys would mop up the chairs I still had my doubts over the machinery. I was not wrong. Their very age rendered them by and large obsolete. I just hoped the scrap metal bidders were in attendance. J. Clifford Atkins was in charge of the sale and I stood at his side to take down the buyers' names and the hammer price.

'Lot 1: the tube-forming machine. Where will you start me – four hundred pounds?'

Silence. That was not unusual; there is always silence when an auctioneer asks for an opening bid. In this instance, however, it was not due to tactics but a complete and genuine lack of interest.

'Three hundred then. Two hundred anywhere?'

Silence.

'One hundred's a start then.'

He turned to me and, in a whisper, shouted in my ear, 'Has anyone bid yet?'

I shook my head. Like many deaf people Cliff forgot that not everyone had the same level of hearing as himself and that he didn't need to shout.

'Fifty ... twenty ... ten pounds – surely?'

When he asked for £20 a number of voices shouted yes but Cliff didn't hear them; when he dropped down to £10 three hands shot up simultaneously and another Cliffism came forth: 'Now you all want it!'

This was not strictly true but at least it conveyed to the bidders that there was a modicum of competition between them. The bidding crept up.

'Ten, twelve, fifteen, eighteen, twenty, twenty-two, twenty-five, twenty-eight.'

Twenty-eight pounds for a machine that over the years must have earned a fortune for its owners until the chair gravy train came to a sticky end. It was sold to the man in the shiny suit and his large daughter with the sheepskin slippers. They bought not only this lot but every other that failed to reach £50: a figure I later found out was their maximum. In this instance they bought nearly every lot of machinery. The sale moved further into the warehouse and we left behind the machinery that had already been sold. I couldn't help but notice Shiny Suit had backed his rusting old pick-up next to the lots he had bought, almost as if he were afraid someone might steal them. I watched out of the corner of my eye, intrigued to see how he would move some of the lumps I had struggled with. He didn't move any: he just walked away and in stepped his daughter. She rolled the grubby cardigan up, crouched down and picked up a machine like a Russian weightlifter attempting the clean and jerk. The machine was lifted straight off the floor in one movement and was thrown over the sides of the pickup. I could hardly believe what I had seen. Her father was nonchalantly talking to the other scrap dealers while she moved among the machinery, hurling her father's purchases on to the pick-up truck. She was obviously not a lady to argue with, nor would I have fancied playing rugby against her. All the time she was loading the truck her father and the others ignored her as they chatted amiably.

Meanwhile we had started to sell the office chairs.

'One hundred, one twenty, one fifty, one eighty, two hundred.'

And on the bidding went with the first lot of six chairs selling for £320. The competition among the dealers was strong and the following lots of chairs all made similar amounts of money.

Cliff was a good auctioneer once he had got into his rhythm but needed the presence of his clerk to act as security in the event of any questions coming from the audience that weren't answered by the stock reply of, 'Right, right, right, jolly good.'

The good nature of this response might have been appreciated but was not much use to a dealer wanting to know which lot number we were on. Most people would have struggled to cope with his disability in a normal job; Cliff, with his usual aplomb, simply ignored it and was very good at what he did.

As we sold more and more of the chairs the sale total started to creep up and was getting close to the £35,000 mark when it became ominously clear that over half the total had been spent by one fairly strange-looking character.

He looked to be seventy or so and was about five feet four inches tall and must have weighed some eight and a half stone. Yet he stood out from the crowd by virtue of his dress. He wore a thick double-breasted black suit with huge lapels and a thick chalk pin-stripe like Cary Grant used to wear in those late forties war films. The trousers were held up by a thick brown belt like a barber's strop while the jacket covered a grubby white crew-neck T-shirt over which our star bidder wore a pink nylon shirt with only the two buttons above the waistband done up. The outfit was topped off by a brown 'Humphrey Bogart' trilby and on his feet he wore the latest pair of Nike trainers.

'Go and find out who he is and how much he's spent. I'll book for myself.'

Cliff thought he had whispered this to me but in reality the whole audience heard his aside. Our man simply smiled and carried on bidding as the next lot was offered. I wandered back to the office where Hinge and Bracket were preparing the accounts at a rate that would embarrass modern-day computers, such was their speed and accuracy.

'Who's buyer number 23 and how much has he spent?' I asked the two ladies, each of whom was flanked by the ever-present cigarette and lemon tea.

'His name's Dick Berry, he says he's a government surplus dealer from Manchester. His bill so far is just over sixteen thousand pounds.'

Back I wandered to where the auction was being conducted. Nothing had changed; our man Dick was still monopolising the bidding.

'His name's Dick Berry, dealer from Manchester, and he's spent about sixteen grand.'

'What?' queried my employer. I loudly repeated the information which drew the same reply. I shouted the information he required so that everyone now knew the identity of our star buyer and exactly how much he had spent.

'Find out if he's good for it,' barked J. Clifford.

Off I wandered again, not quite knowing where I should go to try to obtain an instant credit rating for one Dick Berry. I eventually caught the eye of one of the local dealers I knew and who I guessed might know the identity of the mystery buyer. I was also well aware that he had a loud and colourful turn of phrase.

'He only bloody wants to bloody know if Dick bloody Berry's blood sound. Bloody hell. Sound, bloody sound, he could buy the whole bloody sale. Course he's bloody sound.'

I passed this information on to the only person in the warehouse who hadn't heard it. His response was predictable: 'Jolly good, right, right, right, right. Bid me, Mr Berry – three fifty for the next lot.'

By the end of the sale Dick Berry had spent nearly £42,000. He walked up to Hinge and Bracket in the office and took out a huge, flat wad of notes from enormous pockets in his trousers which seemed to start at the waistband and reach to below the knee. They needed to be capacious for the amount of money Dick Berry carried. Hinge and Bracket counted out the correct money and gave him back part of the pile of cash. He walked over to me, smiled, and said, 'My lorry will be here in the morning, young sir.'

I watched as he walked out to a top-of-the-range Mercedes-Benz motor car. He climbed into the passenger seat and was driven off.

I later discovered from my local 'bloody' dealer friend that Dick Berry started out life as a rag and bone man in Manchester. Through long hours and hard graft he had climbed up the ladder and had become one of the country's top government surplus dealers. There was very little that he would not try to deal in and his skill was in buying the most bizarre lots at a price that he could turn into a profit. He could not drive, never having passed his test, and was driven around the countryside to all the sales in his Merc by his next-door neighbour's son.

A ritual, or rather a pantomime developed at future sales: Dick would carefully view the lots on offer and then come and seek me out. 'Will that buy it, young sir?' he would say as he pulled out an enormous bundle of notes from his trouser pocket. I'd laugh and tell him that we had to go ahead with the sale. Out would come the wad from the other pocket. 'Well, what about that, young sir?'

My local ministry dealer friend later told me that Dick used to carry £25,000 in each pocket. Fifty thousand pounds was more than the price of a house in those days.

I was sorely tempted, just once, to take the money and answer, 'Jolly good, right, right, right.'

Lot 9

Mrs T's Plates

It took nearly seven years for me eventually to dedicate my working life to the world of fine art and antiques. Certainly they weren't always fine nor necessarily antique but at last I could specialise in looking at the little bits of our past that so fascinated me. My particular interest centred on pieces that told us something of the way we lived in the past and also of the people whose hands they had passed through. Handling these clients was sometimes trickier, for not all were as charming as the Slaters at Burton Hall had been and whose pieces had inspired my choice of direction. But they were all characters, and certainly added to the variety of my life – and kept me away from cattle markets.

It would have been about 1985 that I found myself standing on the doorstep of a lady who was a character in the extreme.

'Are you the orkshunhear or the gars man?'

I was on my way to an appointment in the countryside and decided to fit in a call that I had been putting off for a long while. I had first met her many years ago with Mr Rayer. A master of understatement, he had described her as mildly eccentric. Mrs Thompson was, quite simply, crackers. Over the years I had looked at everything from Regency rosewood tables to plastic washing-up bowls. She was forever trying to find something in her home to sell that would augment the rather meagre services pension that she lived on. Her opening line about me being the auctioneer or the gasman was, I think, an attempt at humour. She certainly laughed after she said it, in a way that came perilously close to shaking out her slightly loose-fitting dentures (they almost might not have been made for her). Her father had been an army brigadier, but if he had been a military genius he had clearly not been a financial one. Her husband, a slightly lower ranking officer, had not shared her father's acumen in either respect, so there was no money left. Previous generations of the Thompson clan, however, had been astute collectors with a good eye. Most of these gems had long since been sold, and now we were scraping the barrel.

Mrs Thompson was the closest thing I'd

ever seen to a living pantomime dame. She had a huge, immaculately coiffured mass of grey hair that looked for all the world like a wig and more make-up than a circus clown. But her most striking feature was her lipstick. It looked as if it had been put on with a three-inch paintbrush, almost touching the edge of her nostrils at the top, and at the bottom nearly reaching her chin. And in the middle of this great big blood-red target were her sloppy teeth. They moved around in a way that bore no relation to the words that emanated from them, rather like a film where the lip movements are slightly out of sync. It was strangely hypnotic, but also rendered a conversation with her seriously hard work as you struggled to understand what she said.

The purpose of this visit had originated about three weeks earlier. 'Mrs T', which was one of the ways in which Ella in the office referred to her – the 'Bag Lady' was another – had phoned to ask me to look at a set of eight meat plates. Such plates had been manufactured in the nineteenth century by the major, and minor, china companies in England and in the days of large families would have looked resplendent bearing huge Christmas turkeys or roast joints. We spoke at some length about them. They were now quite collectable, particularly in the American market to where a lot of our antiques are exported.

'Mrs Thompson,' I asked, 'are they by a factory such as Coalport or Doulton?'

'No, dear,' came back the reply.

That was a bit disappointing. I was hoping for a set of plates or chargers by one of the better English factories.

'Well, are they decorated, perhaps with a tiger-hunting scene with elephants, or something similar?'

Common blue and white plates of the nineteenth century had the traditional Willow pattern. Moving up the scale of desirability, some were decorated with Italian landscape scenes where figures fished in ornamental lakes, while those at the top of the range had rarer subjects such as the one I had asked about. Some of these scarcer ones could be worth hundreds of pounds each, or perhaps even more to a collector.

'No, dear.'

I was getting rather desperate, but after some of the things Mrs T had had me looking at recently I shouldn't have expected too much.

'Mrs Thompson, is there any decoration at all on them?'

'No, dear.'

Hell, I was doomed. Plain white dinner plates were worth, on a good day with a following wind, about £5 to £10 each. The trouble with Mrs T was that, like a lot of people, I suppose, if I told her that her goodies were worth a fortune I was obviously good at my job, whereas if I indicated that they were not worth selling I got, 'Perhaps they're not your area, dear. Should I take them to a specialist?'

She never did, or if so she must have got the same advice, for whenever I visited her all the items I had marked down as saleroom rejects were scattered around her home. As you entered the house you were hit by the most overpowering smell of boiling cabbage. Over the years I had varied my visiting time to try to avoid the smell but it seemed to be an all-day operation. The wallpaper, which had been hung since the 1920s, had curious outlines all over it, showing where a lovely little watercolour had once hung, or a Georgian longcase clock had stood. The stencil-like effect had been caused not only by age but also by half a century of nicotine staining from the sixty untipped cigarettes that Mrs T consumed every day. I used to smoke until I met Mrs T, or, more importantly, went to her house. It wasn't that they had affected her health – she must have been pushing eighty, yet seemed as fit as a butcher's whippet – but the colour of the walls. They were a sticky yellow. There were watercolours that couldn't be seen under the fog of exhaled tobacco that had congealed on the glass. Pictures of Mrs T's front room would have had a far greater effect on the lungs of the nation's smokers than any government health warnings.

The family home was quite a modest town house in Worcester and Mrs T was a fairly regular sight walking into the city to do her shopping. She was always accompanied on these trips by a failing supermarket bag – hence Ella's other name for her – although what she carried in it no one knew. Presumably cabbages and lipstick.

Anyway, here I was at her front door. We exchanged pleasantries and I picked up the thread of our telephone conversation – I knew I would have to remind her why I was there. 'Morning, Mrs Thompson, I've come to look at your meat plates.'

'Pardon, dear?' she said. Or at least I think that's what she said, but with her teeth it sounded more like 'Garden here.'

'You've got some meat plates,' I repeated.

'Yes, I know,' she said. This was going to be a long hard job. 'I was going to call you because I wanted to sell them,' she went on.

'Well, that's fortunate, I'm glad I called by,' I said. 'While I'm here I may as well have a look at them.'

'Now you're here you may as well have at look at them.'

'Good idea,' I replied.

Mrs T went on, 'They're about this big' – holding her hands apart until some thirty inches separated them – 'and as well as the eight plates I've got the two strainers as well.' Eventually we made our way from the front doorstep into the hall.

Still dreading the sight of eight grubby white and chipped china meat plates, I asked the question again, hoping that they would have miraculously sprouted some sort of pattern since we had last spoken. 'Is there no decoration of any sort on them or perhaps even a factory mark?'

Back came the reply I anticipated. 'No dear. They're really very plain with no marks at all,' she went on, 'except the hallmarks.'

'*Hallmarks?*' I exclaimed, somewhat staggered.

'Yes,' came back Mrs T. 'Doesn't all silver have hallmarks on it?'

Well, I couldn't argue with that. Indeed it does. My £100 set of scrubby white dinner plates had suddenly turned into a good set of Victorian silver plates. How good would they be? I wondered with a surge of optimism.

'Perhaps I'd better have a look.'

Mrs T vanished and reappeared with an armful of plates. They were loosely wrapped in what looked like the *Daily Sketch* of about 1940 – very yellowing newsprint with reports of the war. When I unwrapped them my first thought was that they looked like gold. I then realised this was the coating that

Mrs T's lungs had deposited. Somewhat gingerly I took the plates in my hand and started to look for the marks. I was half convinced they were plate and would not carry the hallmarks that would confirm that they were silver.

Wrong again. Bright, clear hallmarks giving the year of make, 1852, shown by an old English letter 'Q'; the hallmark of the assay office – a leopard's head signifying London, and a lion looking sideways which indicated that they were indeed silver; and finally the letters 'EB' and 'JB', the mark of the silversmiths, the Barnards. Marks such as these are punched into any silver object and, with the appropriate reference books, tell you all you need to know.

'Mrs Thompson, these really are rather good,' I said, trying to get the treacly brown slime from the plates off my hands. 'There should be a good demand for these in the saleroom and with some luck they should make over five thousand pounds.'

'Splendid, I knew they were good. Father bought them from a dealer in Brighton just before the war.' At least I think that's what she said, but with her teeth I had to do some guessing. Mrs T's house was so cluttered that the plates had been hidden somewhere over the years, and Mrs T's mind resembling her house meant that she had forgotten about them. Their reappearance was due to what she described as 'a bit of spring cleaning'. The reality, I suspect, was that she had been searching through the tea chests that were dotted around the already jumbled house. She once explained to me that she came from a family of hoarders and these chests represented her inheritance from various members of her now deceased family, including her father. Most of the chests now contained only yellowing paper and unsaleable tat, the good stuff having long since been sold by me and my predecessors, but not all of them had been thoroughly searched.

I asked Mrs T how much her father had paid for them and although she couldn't remember exactly she thought it was about £100. Seemingly not a bad return, but that was a huge sum of money in those days.

The auction duly came. This was one sale where I definitely did not want the vendor in the room. Mrs T was like a puppy: you were never sure whether she was going to lick your hand or do something unmentionable on the carpet.

All the silver buyers had left the London silver vaults where they did their business and had made the trip to Worcestershire. To hear them talk you would think that Worcester was somewhere between Outer Mongolia and Siberia. The jungle drums had worked again. As local dealers see the catalogues they start ringing the more important dealers and so word is passed around. The auctioneer's other ploy is to place an advert in the trade paper and wait for the reactions. The collectors and dealers will ring in the week prior to the sale, all searching for goods fresh to the market and Mrs T's plates were very much new to the saleroom.

By the time the plates came up for sale, the saleroom was packed, and as is usual when a good lot is offered an expectant hush took over the room. The bidding was frenetic and quickly soared through my pre-sale £5,000 estimate. It reached about £7,000 then slowed down; it was between one of the London dealers and a private collector. Bidding wars are a battle of nerves and all sorts of tactics are employed. The dealer tried every trick in the book to put off the collector, all quite legitimate.

'Which lot are we on, sir?' was his opening gambit in the battle of the bidders. The seasoned auction-goer will want to dictate the pace of the bidding rather than let the auctioneer try to sweep everyone along with the bids coming fast and furious. As a rough rule of thumb the more time a bidder has to think, the more doubts that creep in.

'Can you guarantee the hallmarks, sir?' was his next shot and was designed to raise uncertainty about the authenticity of the plates in the opposition's mind. Our collector was undeterred.

The dealer slowed the bidding down even more, shook his head and said loudly, 'No more, sir, too dear,' and then bid again when the collector was not put off.

After a hard, long-drawn-out battle we eventually got up to just over £9,000 and the dealer simply shook his head and walked out of the room. The collector had won the day.

Some three weeks after the sale Ella, in the front office, rushed into my room to tell me that a very excited Mrs T was waiting for me. As she hadn't attended the sale she had had no idea of the results until my cheque had dropped through her letterbox.

She was almost overcome with emotion and as well as my usual fee I got a grateful, if somewhat terrifying, kiss from her. I think she may just have bought a new shade of lipstick with part of her sale proceeds.

Lot 10

Hilary's China

'I'm sure he said his name was Hilary,' came the voice down the phone.

Ella, who ran my Worcester office, was normally good with names. All the girls were really switched on, especially when it came to details like the gender of a client. In fact if ever a flaw revealed itself in the organisational skills of my business, it was normally down to me.

'It's either a man and I've got his name wrong, or it's a lady with a really deep voice,' she continued. I thought I'd better take the call.

'Good morning, Philip Serrell speaking,' I replied in a voice that I hoped didn't sound too much like I was taking a hamburger order.

'Hello there, sorr,' came the response. The accent was very thick and almost Irish. 'It's 'bout me choyna.'

This was going to be hard work. 'I'm sorry,' I said, totally unaware what the man, or lady with a very deep voice, was referring to.

'Me name's Hilary, sorr, an' it's 'bout me choyna.'

'I'm sorry,' I repeated, not having the first idea what he, for that's what I'm sure it was on the other end of the phone, was talking about.

'Sorry, sorr, wat are yer sorry 'bout, sorr?'

Basically I was beginning to feel sorry that I'd ever taken the call.

'I didn't mean I was sorry as such, only that I was sorry I hadn't understood what you meant.' I was digging myself into a huge hole.

'It's 'bout me choyna, sorr.'

I thought I'd better take this slowly. 'What china's that then?'

'The stuff thay make at the factree, sorr.'

The light was slowly beginning to appear at the end of the tunnel – I just hoped it wasn't another train. My newfound friend, Hilary, was referring to porcelain that was produced by the local Royal Worcester factory. The factory was founded in 1751 by a Dr John Wall and through companies like Flight and Barr, Chamberlains, Grainger and Hadley, all of whom were either direct-line descendants of the original company or had amalgamated with it through the years, its wares had graced royal tables throughout the world – and still do. It was, and is, highly collectable.

'Do you mean Worcester porcelain?'

'Yes, sorr, the choyna stuff,' came back the reply. At last we were beginning to speak the same language.

'Do you think it's old?' I asked.

'Oooh yes, sorr, very old.' This was beginning to sound hopeful. There are some serious collectors of early Worcester porcelain of the eighteenth century and it is very valuable. Hilary followed it up with, 'It must be. Me grandmam gave it to me mam, 'n' she gave it to me.'

Well, that meant it might be as young as about forty years old – not quite the old I had envisaged, but a lot of people seem to

144

think that ownership by a granny means old. The problem now was to try to find out exactly what it was. I normally asked some basic questions over the phone but with Hilary I thought this would be a nonstarter.

'Where are you calling from?' I asked, which drew a rather unusual response.

'In a lay-by outsider Evershum, sorr.'

Evesham is a small town about twelve miles from Worcester, the Vale of Evesham being a market gardening area famed for its asparagus. I wasn't sure which lay-by he was talking about, but I felt that the only way forward was to ask Hilary to bring his china into the office for me to have a look at. So I asked him to come in the following day at about eleven o'clock. From the voice I was convinced my new client was male, but, like Ella, I had clearly heard the name Hilary. As Ella remarked later it was entirely possible that Hilary would appear wearing a skirt. Mind you, in this day and age that was still not necessarily the deciding factor.

By 10.45 a.m. the next day there was a certain amount of excitement in the air. What was the china going to be like? And, perhaps more interestingly, what was Hilary going to be like?

The offices in Worcester are at the end of a terrace, in a converted town house. The neighbouring houses are all occupied by city professionals. Quite what they must have thought when at 10.55 a.m. a terribly rusty van pulled into the courtyard car park, I dread to imagine. And then out climbed Hilary.

Hilary was, most definitely, a *him*. He was about thirty-five and six feet three inches tall. He had a very muscular frame, almost like a bare-knuckle boxer. His most striking feature was his head. It was completely shaved with prominent veins, rather like a cross between a road map and a pickled walnut. Working down, he had huge single earring in his left ear and a spider's web tattoo around his neck. We were in the middle of a warm spell and he had on a vest of the type that marathon runners wear, where the armholes reach down to the waistband. Blue jeans and a pair of steel toecapped market boots completed the picture. Your eyes, however, were constantly drawn back to Hilary's head, and to his mouth where one upper front tooth seemed to have grown out of all proportion to the others. It overhung his bottom lip by what seemed like inches. The nearest thing to Hilary I have ever seen is Plug from the Bash Street Kids in the *Beano*.

'Good morning,' I ventured. I still wasn't sure whether Hilary was his surname or Christian name but I was beginning to think it was the latter. One tell-tale clue was the green sun strip in the window of his van which was about twelve inches high and bore the name 'HILARY' in nine-inch letters. 'Would you like to come in?'

'Yes, sorr,' came back the answer.

When he walked into the room he looked even more enormous; almost intimidating in fact. He put the box under his arm on the table, and sat down.

We talked for a while, and Hilary confirmed my suspicion that he was one of a large body of travelling people who make their way to Evesham at certain times of the year to help harvest the various crops, including the asparagus. Market gardening has always been very labour-intensive and the farmers hire anybody they can find to get in the harvest. The resultant cross-section of society in the fields was incredibly wide. It ranged from genuine travellers, what you might call gypsies, through Asians and Eastern Europeans, to Oxbridge students. Normally they all worked famously well together, although I do remember one year there was a huge fight in a spring onion field that resulted in police from across the county being called in. Apparently hundreds of people were involved on each side, and it was reported on local radio and TV. I would never have thought that onions could heighten emotions so much.

Hilary, though, more friendly than his appearance suggested, was quiet and it was quite difficult to drag snippets of information from him. He told me he had lived in a village and that he had drunk in the local pub where he had met 'That Richard Branston, now he's a genleman, sorr, you knows 'im.' For a moment I thought Hilary was going to talk to me about pickle, but as the conversation developed I realised who he was talking about. He was keen to tell me about all the famous rock stars he had seen in the pub with 'that music and train feller'. He also told me that he was a true gypsy, something about being the seventh child of the seventh child, which I didn't understand, and suddenly he threw into the conversation: 'That Mick Jagger – I've met him too, sorr.'

When he seemed relaxed enough I thought we had better look at the china he had brought in with him. This was the moment of truth. Hilary was a hulk of a man, but with extraordinary delicacy he started to unpack small cups and saucers which looked incongruous in his huge hands. I took over from him, unwrapping them in wonder. They were clearly rare and I was itching to find out where Hilary had got them from, how long they had been in his family and what he thought they might be worth. Perhaps the $64,000 question for me was would Hilary want to sell them. As I pulled another cup out Hilary remarked, 'That Richard Keith – I've met him too, sorr.'

When we had finished unpacking the box I was presented with a cased set of six Royal Worcester coffee cups and saucers. They were in a lovely velvet-lined box and contained the original hallmarked silver spoons that had been exquisitely enamelled. The crowning glory was that each cup and saucer was decorated with very rich hand-painted fruit. The set had been produced, I would guess, some time in the 1950s and the artists who had painted it had signed each piece.

'Well,' I said, 'that's really wonderful.'

'I know,' said Hilary, 'I've met 'em all, and due know, theym normal people, jus like you 'n' me.'

I knew that travelling people collected china and glassware but I had never had any of them come to me to sell any before. There are two particular types of porcelain: Royal Worcester hand-painted fruit and Royal Crown Derby decorated with the Imari pattern (this is a design of oriental origins). Both of these wares were highly decorative and collectable. Apparently Hilary's grandmother and mother had collected Royal Worcester pieces over the years, like countless other travellers of their generation. Banks and building societies didn't feature too high on the list of recommended investments for travellers; it was porcelain like this that they put their money into, knowing that it could always be sold and converted into hard cash when required. I knew from my little experience of dealing with travellers that it never did to enquire too much, certainly when it came to money. Talking to Hilary it became clear that what was unpacked before me was only the tip of the iceberg.

His family now apparently wanted to raise some cash, perhaps to buy one of those chrome and mirror-bedecked caravans that they lived in, or a van to pull it. The family would have met and, having decided to sell the collection, charged Hilary with dealing with 'the outsider', as I was, being a non-gypsy. The cased coffee cups in front of me were to be a test, to see if I was up to the job. I felt if I could do a good job with these, I would gain the family's trust and then, who knew, more might follow. There was, however, an underlying mystery – I certainly hadn't been given the full picture. Hilary's cards were clasped firmly to his considerable chest and I was going to have to build up a lot of trust with him if, as an outsider, I was going to be taken into his confidence.

I have to say the cased set would not prove to be the biggest challenge to my auctioneering career. They were highly desirable and, provided I did a proper job promoting them on my website and through the specialist press, should make a good sum of money.

By the time the sale came around we had telephone lines booked by a number of collectors and dealers including one in New York and another in Australia. This was in addition to a large number of people in the audience. Just before the set came up for auction, there was a rustle of movement at the door, and the genteel atmosphere of the saleroom was suddenly disturbed. Enter Hilary, wearing his 'toe-tector' boots, and looking as if he had just finished ploughing a field with his bare hands. The weather was still very hot and, in polite terms, Hilary was not so gently glowing. To say his presence was overpowering is to put it mildly, particularly within the somewhat judgemental antique world. As I watched from the rostrum, I could see my clients shifting uncomfortably in their seats. Hilary strode noisily to the front of the saleroom. Of course, they needn't have worried.

''Ello there, sorr,' boomed the huge voice. 'Be sure you gets a gud price for 'em.'

If anything was going to encourage people to bid it was the thought of Hilary being there hoping for a 'gud price'.

The estimate on the set was between £1,200 and £1,800. Hilary had said before the auction the family would be delighted with anything over £1,000. The bidding started at £1,500 with fierce competition between the man on the telephone in New

York and an English collector in the room. The latter eventually won out at £3,200. Hilary was over the moon. As the hammer came down he shouted out, 'Well done, sorr.'

That's certainly something that's never happened while I was actually selling, either before or since. The reaction of the rest of the audience was fascinating. Hilary, with those three words, had ceased to be the intimidating character they had at first thought him to be. It was almost as if they had felt they needed to protect me from this ruffian intruder into the world of antiques. Now the warmth of his praise seemed to have convinced everyone that he was no threat to me; and his delight in his sale result permeated to everyone else in the saleroom, so that I have never had such a contented set of buyers and sellers. I was confident I would now get the rest of Hilary's collection.

We normally send payment out by post, but obviously having a lay-by in Evesham as a postal address would present Her Majesty's Mail with a few problems. So some weeks later he came in to collect the cheque and told us how pleased the whole family was with the price I had achieved. I left it at that, and thought that I would wait for him to contact me about selling the rest of the collection. I was also hoping to find out how the name Hilary came about. Well,

I'm still waiting. I suppose the nature of a travelling family is that they do travel around. Maybe Hilary will appear again as suddenly as he did before and some of those gypsy mysteries may be shared with me.

Lot 11

A Vintage Sale

The Hyde twins had eked out a living on their small-holding for over fifty years. The twins were unusual in that they did not own their farm – it was tenanted – and their only assets lay in their implements and stock. They rented the property from the local lord of the manor and although they were under no pressure from him to give up their tenancy, they were now nearing seventy and felt the time had come to retire to a quieter life in a small bungalow in the centre of the village where they had lived all their lives. They had never married and there was no succeeding generation to hand on their tenancy to. Being identical twins, they had come to a unanimous decision, apparently independently, but simultaneously. Every-one knew of the Hyde twins; they were rarely ever apart, worked all the hours God

153

sent and lived a very frugal life. Rumour had it that their home paid scarcely a nod to the comforts of late twentieth-century living; the farmhouse and buildings, implements and farming practices were straight out of a museum of rural life.

They stood out among the farming fraternity in one other respect – they were the only identical lady twins I knew who had dedicated their lives to farming. They only left their holding, the tenancy of which had been passed down to them by their father, to travel into the village or the county town itself. I assumed the ladies had been christened with forenames but no one seemed to know what these were. Certainly they were known to everyone as Miss, or the Misses Hyde and referred to each other as 'my sister'.

Both ladies drove a Morris thousand traveller estate, identical in colour, year and model, but as they went everywhere together the one Miss Hyde drove her car on week-days and the other Miss Hyde used her car as their Sunday-best vehicle. I first knew of their intention to sell up when the weekday Morris pulled into the car park by our office. The ladies had telephoned to make an appointment to see me. They gave no indication of what the business was that they wanted to discuss; with the Misses Hyde certain formalities had to be observed. The appointment was duly made and would be the time to discuss the matter; it certainly would not do to broach it over the telephone.

The two ladies were ushered into my office and asked if they would like a cup of tea. The girls in the office had strict instructions not to bring out our usual mugs but to use the best china cups and saucers. The ladies had dressed up for their trip to what they regarded as the big city. On the farm they both wore identical apron-front boiler suits of the type that painters and decorators wear. Their work outfits were finished off with crisply ironed shirts and matching black army-style boots. All this had been discarded and the ladies would not have looked out of place on the local Women's Institute annual outing. Pleated tartan skirts with razor-sharp ironing lines, round-neck cardigans and sensible brogue shoes were the order of the day. The ladies' make-up budget over the last seventy years would not have exceeded £10: their faces were scrubbed clean.

'Mr Serrell, we have considered our position and have decided to retire from the farm,' the first Miss Hyde said.

'Sadly there's little of value but we would appreciate your help to sell the machinery and the like,' said the second Miss Hyde; it was almost as if they had rehearsed the conversation, each taking alternate lines.

It was a long time since I had visited their farm but knew of its reputation as not being the most up to date in the district.

'We are not even sure there will be enough to cover your fee,' said the first, with the second completing the sentence, 'an eventuality we have taken account of.'

I told the ladies I would be delighted to help and made an appointment to see them the following week. It was a sunny spring morning as I drove into the farm. The whole yard in front of the house was bordered with old cast-iron pig troughs and ancient stone pump troughs that looked a picture, each overflowing with a glorious display of flowers. I walked to the front porch and gently tapped the polished brass lion's mask knocker that adorned the front door. The ladies arrived together to greet me; it was a work day and the Misses Hyde were suitably attired in their farming overalls.

'Good morning, Mr Serrell, so kind of you to come; do come in and have some tea,' they said, almost in unison.

We walked through into the front room and tea was served. I can remember some occasions with Mr Rayer when a farm visit like this resulted in the whisky bottle being brought out. I would imagine the Hyde twins' only concession to alcohol was a bottle of sherry at Christmas. Their home was spotlessly clean and without a pin out of place.

The drawing room where we were sitting had flowers everywhere; but what really struck the eye were the furnishings. No antiques as such, just sensible pieces, very dated. There was no room for a television in this house, merely a huge old-fashioned radio around which I've no doubt they both sat to listen to *The Archers*.

'We have told our landlord of our intentions and he has given us permission to hold an auction sale here. We would like you to sell everything that you possibly can; our worry is that we will have to pay to dispose of our old machinery – not that there is too much of it.'

I suggested to the ladies that we should wander around and see exactly what the job entailed. They were most concerned about troubling me and continued to apologise as we walked towards the covered buildings.

I opened the big timber door and the day's bright sunshine lit up the contents. And what an extraordinary sight was revealed. It's not just antique furniture and fine art that have appealed to me over the years; I've also always been captivated by old things that tell a story. There were four such things in this Worcestershire farm barn.

Mr Hyde, the ladies' father, had grown vegetables on the farm during his tenure and apparently he had been renowned for delivering his produce throughout the area with his lorry. It was a 1930s Bedford four-wheel lorry painted in a rich green livery with a scrolling name plate over the cab proclaiming, 'Hyde's Vegetables & Produce' in vivid red old English text. Parked next to it were two lovely old tractors. The first was a Ferguson Brown, a forerunner of the well-known 'Grey Fergie' used on so many of the local farms, and the second was a bright orange Allis Chalmers. My father, coming from a farming family, had become an avid collector of ancient lorries and tractors – every outbuilding at home seemed to house the things – so I recognised these as real gems. They were all original and had never had a coat of fresh paint but had been lovingly used by their owner; no doubt things of joy every time they were driven. The fourth bygone was a massive old stationary engine, almost like a traction engine without the wheels. It had a huge flywheel that was nearly six feet in diameter, the whole machine being about twelve feet wide. It bore the maker's name proudly in letters four inches high: 'Black-stone Oil Engine'. It would originally have been used on the farm to power various smaller machines such as chaff cutters and root slicers by a system of belts, and would have been the central source of power on the farm.

'You look captivated, Mr Serrell.'

The second sister continued, 'Would you

like to see the engine run?'

Without waiting for an answer, both ladies walked over to the engine and started a pre-ignition sequence that mission control at Houston would have been proud of. Eventually it fired; the huge wheel turned agonisingly slowly; just when it seemed like the engine would stall there was a deep 'borf' noise, a plume of smoke and the wheel turned for another long, slow revolution until the process was repeated again. Simple, but I could have stood and watched the wheel go round for hours, waiting almost hypnotised for each cycle to begin.

'They are really part of the family and we have never thought of them in monetary terms. In fact we were not too sure if anyone would be interested in buying them.'

Well, I was guessing, but I thought that not only would these four generate a great deal of interest but the sale total for them could be in excess of £10,000.

We walked around the rest of the buildings and while there was nothing to rival the tractors, lorry and engine in terms of value, interesting bits of farm history lay everywhere. Nothing seemed to be newer than about thirty years old; there was a wonderful old lawnmower, a sheep shearer that was driven by a hand-turned wheel, and old vegetable spraying syringes – all of them, as rumour reported, museum-like exhibits on a working farm.

'Do you think there is enough here for a sale?' one twin asked.

I nodded my head enthusiastically. I felt that a sale on a Saturday would be the best bet. It wouldn't be a massive sale, only about 200 to 250 lots, but given a following wind there should be a good result.

The twins seemed to show little curiosity about the value of the items they were selling, only concern that they would not be left with vast amounts to clear. They were also anxious that no one would turn up to their sale. I was sure neither of these would be a problem.

I have always been of the view that I would rather be criticised for over-advertising a sale rather than under-advertising. Accordingly, adverts were placed not only in the local papers but also in the specialist magazines and journals for collectors who might be interested in the Hyde twins' belongings. I told the sisters that we might be spending as much as £1,000 on advertising and they were horrified. They thought this was as much as the sale would bring them in total and it was a task to convince them otherwise. Sure enough, as soon as the adverts came out the telephone started to ring; and ring and ring. The interest was phenomenal and came from all over the country. It wasn't just potential customers who were on the phone either – the Misses Hyde contacted me fairly regularly to express their ongoing worry that no one would come to the sale and what on earth would they do with what was left.

They needn't have been anxious. The Saturday of the sale duly came and I drove to the farm at about seven thirty. I'd decided not to have any viewing on the day before the sale but only on the morning of the sale itself. My reason for this was simple: I felt that if people were only allowed to come on the sale day they might not leave after viewing but would linger, possibly just out of curiosity, and might end up bidding on one of the lots on offer. The road to the sale was like a car park. Viewing was not due to start until eight thirty and already there were droves arriving early. What was all the more pleasing was that many of the vehicles that had spilled over from the lane into the field opposite had travelled from all over the country. Even better, a lot of the vans, lorries and cars had trailers hitched up behind; this meant they had come to buy and had the equipment to take their purchases home with them. I walked into the barn where my four star lots were stored and saw hordes swarming over them. Many were wearing sweatshirts proclaiming their allegiance to one tractor, engine and lorry club or another. Some days, as an auctioneer, you know all is going to go well; this was one of those days.

I decided to go to the house and seek out the twins. They were dressed in their best weekend attire and were busily comforting themselves that it would soon be over.

The sale was due to start at ten thirty prompt; I had learned a lot from Mr Rayer but for me the advertised time for a sale to start was sacrosanct and not a basis for negotiation as it had been with him. The hour arrived and the sale started with the lesser lots.

The sheep shearer sold for £55 and the old lawnmower was bid to a startling £260. The twins followed me around as the lots were sold and each time the hammer came down it elicited remarks such as, 'Well I never,' from the first and, 'Goodness me,' in retort from the second.

The last four lots were the highlight of the sale. My father had told me that my initial estimate of £10,000 was a little conservative; he was a careful man and if he thought it was conservative we should do really well. He thought the last two lots, the Ferguson Brown and the Blackstone engine, should sell particularly well as they were both rare and avidly sought after by collectors. First up was the Allis Chalmers tractor.

'Bid me two thousand pounds someone?'
Silence.

'Oh dear!' cried both the ladies.

The audience and I all knew that it was going to make over this figure but the customary sale drama had to be acted out and this entailed starting as low as possible. Eventually some wag at the back shouted out, 'Five hundred pounds – 'as it got any warranty?'

'No, but you should have – at least it's a start.'

On the bidding went until the hammer fell at £3,200 to a man wearing an Allis Chalmers sweatshirt, underbid by another similarly attired. They had both shown their hands by their clothes. At this point a smile developed on the ladies' faces and I heard a relieved whisper: 'At least that should cover our costs.'

'Lot 223: the Bedford lorry. Where will you start me?'

I hoped it might make £4,000 and was pleased to have an opening bid of £3,000. Another quickly put in a bid and I recognised both the bidders as local vegetable merchants. Neither wanted to be outdone and the lorry sold for £5,800. (Pleasingly, it transpired after the sale that the buyer was going to leave the Bedford just as it was in the Hyde livery colours and take it to display at local shows, a fact that delighted both sisters.)

'Next, gentlemen, the Ferguson Brown.'

The silence lasted longer than normal this time, with eager eyes staring at me and one another in anticipation. An auctioneer is normally delighted to have two bidders on one lot; I had about ten, all trying to bid at the same time for the old tractor. It sold for £15,600.

'I think I need a cup of tea,' I heard the first sister say.

'Last lot of the day: the Blackstone engine. Where this time then?'

The silence now took on extra long proportions.

'Please, bid me?'

Followed by: 'Well, if you don't bid I can't sell it.'

'Three thousand pounds, sir.'

Like all auctioneers I can talk pretty quickly but I had a job to keep up; hands were flying up all over the place and bids were shouted from everywhere. Up it went, £500 at a time, higher and higher, until eventually it sold for £21,000. The buyer was a man I had seen parking a lorry earlier in the day with a Leeds telephone number on the cab door. He hadn't wasted his journey. The second Miss Hyde, clearly almost overcome, capped her sister's request for tea.

'Perhaps we ought to open that bottle of sherry we bought last Christmas, dear.'

Lot 12

One Bid Church

John Church was a funny old stick of about seventy. While you could not describe him as being miserable he was never full of the joys of life. He was a general dealer: he would buy anything that he thought he could make a profit on, but, being as mean as hell, he never bought at the top end of the market. He attended every sale going, the smaller the better – both the local livestock market where he would buy horses and calves, and the fortnightly general sales where, armed with an antique price guide-book, he was a regular. These were sales that dealt with household clearance items and lesser antiques. However his price guide, upon which he relied utterly, was about twelve years out of date. So an item in his book might be marked at £20 when in fact it was now worth £150. This, allied to his general caution about spending money, meant that he was anything but the best buyer in the world. If an auctioneer was struggling to get a bid on a lot at £10 it wouldn't be long before Church spoke up.

The trouble was he had the most horrific stammer, and everyone in the saleroom knew it. This, despite the tiny sums of money involved, always created an air of anticipation before he bid.

'T ... T ... T... T...' Nothing would come out of his mouth. There would be an extraordinary silence as the whole room waited for him. 'T ... T ... T...' he'd continue, until after what seemed a lifetime he eventually spat out, 'T ... T ... Two pounds, sir.' He was known in the saleroom as 'One Bid Church', because that's all he ever had – one bid. It was almost as if the energy involved in getting that one bid out exhausted him so completely he was incapable of continuing. This naturally meant that he didn't buy very much – but if he did it was cheap. Of course there's usually a reason why goods are cheap in a saleroom: because they aren't up to much.

One Bid lived about six miles outside Worcester on a smallholding. All that remained, however, after he had sold off the house and the barns for conversion, was about five acres of land with a mobile home in the corner nearest the road. The whole site was, to be blunt, a complete mess. It was rectangular in shape with the section furthest away from the road fenced off for his stock, which amounted to a few calves and a couple of ponies that were very definitely the runts of their respective litters. A small track led back up towards the mobile home and the road. However, before reaching the mobile home, the track passed a huge pile of wooden pallets surrounding an old tractor with a saw bench at the back. It was here that One Bid used to make unreliable picnic benches, which he tried to sell at car boot sales throughout the county. Anybody who bought one was destined to be pulling splinters out of their behind for the short time the contraption remained upright.

Next stop up the track to the mobile home was what he used to call his implement store. One Bid used to buy any rusting old plough or farm implement in the forlorn hope that he could sell them on for a profit. The reality was that the rusting mass grew ever larger and rustier. Further up the path was a corrugated building that housed One Bid's forays into the antique world, namely three-legged chairs and tables and chests with a drawer missing. This pile was similar to the other two in that it never got any smaller, rather the opposite, and also nothing in the pile ever improved in condition but simply deteriorated as time went by.

The next rather small shed immediately before the mobile home was what One Bid was most notorious for: Horace. Horace was huge with a long shaggy coat and a temperament the wrong side of distinctly unfriendly. He was part Alsatian, part Rott-weiler and a very large part angry elephant with toothache. No one walked past him without taking their life in their hands. I had encountered farm dogs before who adminis-tered a friendly warning nip but Horace was prone to giving a full-blooded bite that rendered medical treatment a necessity.

One Bid had telephoned the office and had asked me to go out to his place to look at a mantel clock he was thinking of selling: apparently he had seen something similar in his reference book. I had tried to get Sophie, who was the saleroom manager, to go out on the call, explaining to her that to further her career in the auctioneering world she had to get used to dealing with all types. An argument I put so well that I almost believed it. But she was having none of it: she had heard about Horace. Well, I had to go and look – in our business you just never know what you're going to find.

I arrived for our appointment about fifteen minutes early, which was most unusual for me but I wanted to get the visit out of the way. I made my way to the door of the mobile home and knocked loudly. Nothing – and best of all not even the usual terrifying growls and barks from Horace. I knocked again; still nothing. I looked down towards the stock field and, past Horace's shed, I could see One Bid in the pile of pallets waving his arms at me and calling. I didn't move – confrontation with Horace was the last thing I wanted, even though he was nowhere to be seen. I stood my ground as One Bid waved his arms and shouted; I couldn't hear a word he said. This small pantomime continued for some minutes and there was still no sign of Horace. I could only think that One Bid was busy and wanted me to go down and see him. I started to walk down the path and the shouting and arm waving became more animated. I began to get a little anxious as I got close to Horace's lair; he might not be around but even so he made me nervous. Horace was a dog that worried people not sheep. I crept past his shed, feeling safer by the step and quite proud of my courage. I was past the point of no return, feeling much more relaxed, when Horace came bounding out of his kennel, and with all his might sank his teeth into my right buttock. It was as if it had been caught in a mantrap. The pain was unbelievable. At last One Bid came rushing up and grabbed Horace by the scruff of the neck, and pulled him off me.

'Mr Church, why the hell did you call me down here?' I cried, trying to stifle the agony, furious that the damn thing had ruined a good pair of trousers.

One Bid shouted back at me, 'I d … d … didn't, I was t … t … t … trying t … t … to t

... t ... tell you n ... n ... not to c ... c ... come d ... d ... down here or the d ... d ... dog would have you.'

And after all that the wretched clock was a typical One Bid lot: the makings – and only the makings – of what once had been a really good clock. Wonderful Regency rosewood case and a quality face with the name of a London make engraved just above the Roman numerals for six o'clock. In good order this would have been worth between £3,000 and £5,000. However, that was as good as it got. On opening the back of the case it became apparent that some vandal had stripped out the original movement and had replaced it with a modern, battery-powered quartz version. Value now: about £300 to £500 for the case alone. I was unsure how to break the news to One Bid – he was as mean as hell but I did quite like him.

'Mr Church,' I started, 'it was once quite a good clock, but now–'

Before I could finish One Bid interrupted me. 'I know, I t ... t ... t ... t ... took it to one of them c ... c ... c ... clock repairers, pa ... pa ... pa ... pathologist I think he said he w ... w ... w ... was.'

I didn't have the heart to butt in and tell him that clock restorers were called horologists.

'He w ... w ... w ... wanted three hundred p

... p ... p ... pounds t ... t ... t ... to restore the old m ... m ... m ... m ... movement and said it w ... w ... w ... w ... w ... would be well worth d ... d ... d ... d ... d ... doing. I kn ... kn ... kn ... knew it wouldn't b ... b ... b ... be worth that sort of m ... m ... m ... m... money and he was trying t ... t ... t ... t ... to do m ... m ... m ... me so I told him to t ... t ... t ... t ... t ... take out the m ... m ... m ... m ... m ... movement and put a n ... n ... n ... n ... n ... new one in. Too clever for 'im, I w ... w ... w ... w ... was,' chuckled One Bid.

I tentatively asked One Bid what he had done with the old movement, hoping that it was somehow salvageable. This was a case where the parts definitely did not equal the sum of the whole. The response from One Bid was so ironically predictable.

'I was t ... t ... t ... too sharp for that p ... p ... p ... p ... pathologist. I reckoned he th ... th ... th ... thought it was worth a few quid so I p ... p ... p ... put it into a sale in Birmingham. They'm cheaper than you,' he delighted in telling me, 'an' it m ... m ... m ... made three hundred sm ... sm ... sm ... smackers,' said One Bid, smiling. Three hundred pounds for the movement alone.

Rather than give me the parts of the clock to sell it transpired that One Bid had taken the movement to a firm of auctioneers in Birmingham who were renowned for cutting their rates. By driving a round trip of eighty-five miles and taking some three hours over the exercise One Bid had saved himself 2 per cent commission, about £6. Well, so be it, I thought.

'The clock complete would have been worth over three thousand pounds. Now it's worth about three hundred.' And then I twisted the knife in with a remark that I later felt bad about: 'Still, you managed to save yourself a bit on the commission.'

One Bid looked so wounded that I instantly felt a strange guilt that I am sure would not have been forthcoming if the boot had been on the other foot. Poor old One Bid – the ultimate case of penny wise, pound foolish.

Lot 13

The Wuster Beards

'Eer, I wanner sell some of those wuster beards.'

This was the opening gambit in a telephone conversation with a new client that had me driving to inspect his collection. The 'wuster beards' were in fact a collection of limited edition birds that were produced by the Royal Worcester porcelain factory in the 1970s. The birds were not the small variety that sat on the mantelpiece but were lifesize models of the differing birds in their natural foliage and habitat. Each model was raised on a wooden plinth and came with a framed certificate of authenticity. They were impressive and expensive pieces of ceramic sculpture that were modelled by one of the twentieth century's foremost modellers, a lady by the name of Dorothy Doughty. Her sister, Freda, was perhaps more prolific in that she was responsible for the small studies of children that were produced by Royal Worcester in various charming series such as the 'Days of the Week' and 'Months of the Year'. Dorothy modelled on a much grander scale. Her studies were not for the mass market, made in many thousands as were Freda's, but were limited to production runs of between 250 and 750. The price altered accordingly: Freda's little figures sold for tens of pounds while her sister's bird studies sold, when new, for many hundreds and sometimes thousands of pounds.

The telephone conversation was with a Liverpudlian with a broad accent who went on to explain that he had three single bird studies and four of the models that were manufactured in pairs. As a firm we had always specialised in the wares from the local Worcester factory and it was not unusual for potential clients to ring from all over the United Kingdom and even occasionally from abroad. I've never been very good at looking at dates in diaries and had made this appointment for the next available Monday, without realising that it was a bank holiday. There is a direct route from Worcester to Liverpool but it's via the M6; and bank holiday Monday and M6 motorway are of course two phrases that do not sit well together. However, it was a busy time at the saleroom and even though it was a public holiday I had decided that I wouldn't change the appointment as it would save valuable hours later on in the week.

As soon as I got going on that Monday morning I began to regret my decision. I'm not sure who designs the signs that they put over motorways but they get it comprehensively wrong. When it flashes, 'Caution Queue Ahead!' you are already in it; when it says, '50 mph' you are crawling along at a snail's pace; and when it says, '40 mph', or even worse, '30 mph' you are more than likely parked in the fast lane. I was at the third stage of these phrases and had been for some time. I was beginning to get a little fractious. I did not mind using a bank holiday to see a client about new business but I did not want to spend it at a standstill on a motorway. I had left home at eight o'clock for the ten thirty appointment but my arrival on time was looking more remote than it normally did. A twelve o'clock arrival was more likely; I thought it best to contact the client from my car phone and let him know of my delay and estimated time of arrival.

'Eer, no worries, we noreezy to find, give us a call when you're close.'

At least the client was relaxed, which was more than could be said for me. The thought of a journey from hell followed by getting lost in a strange city was not brightening my humour. At long last I arrived at the outskirts of Liverpool. I have always been fairly tenacious – some might say stubborn – and decided to try to find my own way to the home of my new client. I eventually found the district that I had been given as an address and, foolishly, thought I was home and dry. Twenty minutes later I had to admit defeat and made the phone call to confess that I was lost.

'Eer, we don' live there.'

'Pardon?' was all I could say.

'Eer, we don' live there.'

'I'm sorry?'

This conversation wasn't going anywhere and was confusing me all the more.

'We live in Toxteth.'

Toxteth is an area of Liverpool that had

made the headlines for the wrong reasons when it experienced what could be described as a certain amount of social disharmony. 'Riots' was the term that newspapers used.

'Eer, if I'd told you we lived in Toxteth you wouldn't have come.'

Well, that was not necessarily true but I could appreciate the logic. I was then given fresh directions which I followed, making my way without mishap until I reached the district of Toxteth. I was looking for number 27 Valentine Road. After the day I had experienced to date I should have guessed that the houses in Valentine Road would have been numbered by someone who either drew them out of a hat or used a pin and a blindfold. Odds and evens were mixed up on both sides and did not run in consecutive order on either side. I was beginning to feel very foolish as I reached for the telephone again.

'I can't seem to find number 27.'

'Eer, our 'ouse don' have a number; it's behind number 12. It's called Donenkay.'

An unusual name for a house, I thought, but none the less I parked outside number 12 and walked around the back to find a bungalow that had been built in a plot at the rear of the other houses. It was styled like a Spanish villa with bright white-painted stucco walls under a red, wavy-tiled roof, and wooden window shutters which were closed and barred. My new client could see me looking quizzically at windows that were shuttered in broad daylight. 'Eer, yer need it round 'ere, it's security. Better be safe not sorry,' he explained later.

To the front of the bungalow was a pair of ornate wrought-iron gates decorated with bright red-painted metal roses. There was a huge reproduction brass bell hanging to one side that I presumed served as a door knocker, with a scrolling gilt house name plate on the other side. I rang the bell and was met by a very cheery chap in his late thirties and a similarly aged lady whom I presumed to be his wife.

'Thanks for comin'. I'm Don 'n' this is me wife, Kay.'

Well, at least that explained something.

We went through a heavily barred front door. Because of the closed shutters, the house was dark inside. This was not helped by deep burgundy paint on the walls and light bulbs that could have been no more powerful than about fifteen watts each. I could hardly see a thing and felt as if I were entering a subterranean world. The decor was certainly not to my taste: once my eyes had accustomed to the gloom I could see glitzy wall lights and chandeliers, all with the same low-wattage bulbs. The walls were lined with garish modern paintings of tropical island views, and reproduction Italian china filled highly gilded reproduction display cabinets. Everything I could see was very expensive, but not overly sought after in the saleroom. Don went on proudly to tell me that he and Kay were partners in a successful discount fitted kitchen business selling throughout the country.

'We werks 'ard 'n' likes to spend our money on nice things. Them beards are in the other room.'

We walked into another room at the rear of the house where, tucked into a cabinet almost as an afterthought, were the works of the great Dorothy Doughty.

'Me mother left 'em to Kay 'n' me 'n' they ain't really our cup o' tea. What d'you think they're worth?' Before I could answer Don said, 'We've got 'em insured for between two and four thousand pounds each.'

Well, that slowed me down a bit. An insurance figure is the replacement value of a particular item and this is normally higher than an expected auction value; sometimes by as much as 50 per cent. My opinion of what these birds might make at auction was considerably lower than the amount they were insured for and I suspected Don and Kay would have second thoughts about selling them.

Before I could say a word Don went on, 'We know they ain't gonna make that kinda money but we don' like 'm 'n' Kay says they gotta go. We might even do better if they broke!'

I was a little relieved by that first remark and told them my valuations, which ranged from £500 to £1,500 each for the single and pairs of models.

'They was 'is mother's pride 'n' joy but they ain't quite fancy enough for us,' Kay went on. 'I like something with a bit of style.'

I resisted a smile and told them that I would be delighted to include them in one of my next sales. I was a bit concerned as to how they would deliver them to a saleroom. Each with their large packing case, they were certainly too big for the Volvo estate and I was going to suggest this was a job for our removal man when Don said, 'We'll get the bloke who delivers our kitchins to bring 'em down to you; 'e's got a job to deliver a kitchin to a lady in the Midlands. It'll save on the bill.'

This made me rather anxious and I explained to Don that an expert was needed to pack and move these models. They were incredibly elaborate and fragile pieces but Don, almost reading my mind, followed on with, 'Eer, 'e's sound, 'e's never damaged a kitchin yet.'

'Don, these really need to be moved by a specialist. They're very delicate and the merest hint of damage will render them practically worthless.'

He would have none of it. Despite my protestations he was adamant that the 'kitchin mover' was the man for the job. There was nothing else I could say or do except take my client's instructions after I had made clear my recommendations.

'Eer, 'ow much is this gonner cost? Will cash 'elp?'

This is an age-old question that every auctioneer has had put to him at one time or another. An auctioneer earns his corn by taking a percentage from the seller and normally the buyer of every lot he sells. This commission is variable depending on the value of the lot, or lots, for sale, but can range between 10 and 17½ per cent on each side. As nearly all salerooms are computerised and thus all records are electronically stored, doing deals for cash has always struck me as foolhardy, and all auctioneers I know take the same view. Added to which I always like to sleep at night and my grandfather's old adage was: never get involved in long conversations with taxmen, doctors, solicitors or policemen. In his experience the only outcome was expense and bad news.

Normally I insist on having goods in the saleroom before cataloguing them and producing the necessary illustrations. In this case I had sold so many of these models that

I had a full library of descriptions and illustrations in the saleroom which I was happy to use for the catalogue. It was time to make the long and tortuous journey home. It was now about four thirty and I set off, dreading the time it would take to get back.

I made my way to the motorway junction and could see the traffic was even heavier than it had been on the journey north. I supposed all the holidaymakers were now driving home; I couldn't see any pleasure in having to endure this sort of travelling torture and calling it a holiday. I decided to motor across country and take some of the back roads. I reasoned that even though it would be a longer journey at least I would be able to keep moving. Soon I was pleased with my decision and was enjoying the countryside; I was making half-decent progress and thought I would make it home by about seven or seven thirty. The thought of a good entry for my next sale and pleasure at not being parked on that three-lane traffic jam lifted my spirits. As I drove on, Donenkay – the people not the house – made me, not for the first time, realise what a fascinating business I was in. It was often remarked that we dealt with everyone from dustmen to dukes, and these two fitted in somewhere in the middle of that broad spectrum. Buyers and sellers alike were a complete cross-section of society.

I was midway between Chester and Shrewsbury in the depths of nowhere, happily musing on the idiosyncrasies of my profession, when I was jolted back to reality by the car developing a mind of its own. For no apparent reason on my part it shot towards the hedge on the nearside at an alarming rate of knots. I slewed to a halt and, a little shaken, got out to find I had had a blow-out of the rear tyre. I was so relieved that I couldn't get the Worcester birds in the back for they would surely all have been damaged.

This would add another half an hour to the trip by the time I had changed the tyre. Jacket off: time to get the spare wheel out; perhaps a fifteen-minute pit stop might just be possible. Typical, I must have taken the socket and wheel-brace out of the car and not put them back; the wretched things were nowhere to be found. I was thankful that my membership to the rescue service was fully paid up; they were after all only a phone call away. I think all mobile phone companies should guarantee network coverage if your car breaks down. Mine simply flashed up the message that said, 'emergency calls only', followed by the 'no network coverage' message. Well, I reckoned this was an emergency – but nothing happened. By the time I had found a public phone it took me nearly two hours to get the recovery van to the side of my car. I foolishly thought all my problems were solved as the van pulled up and out got my knight of the road. He obviously spent a lot of time watching daytime television and antique programmes in particular. Even more specifically the ones that I appeared in.

'Ain't you the bloke off the telly, does them antique programmes?'

'Yes,' I replied. It really is very flattering to be recognised.

'My missus loves you. You always get it wrong!'

That wasn't quite the response I anticipated; to add insult to injury it was followed up with, 'You're a lot shorter in real life, fatter too.'

'Well, they say television adds a few pounds,' I said in my defence.

'Yeah, but not that much. Sorry, mate, I don't mean to be rude – my missus likes big blokes.'

I was relieved to find I had a fan of the fuller frame. All this was most interesting but I just wanted to get my tyre changed. I told him about the missing tools and thought we would be able to get a move on.

'D'you remember that one where you bought that turkey for one hundred and seventy pounds?' This was an episode I had tried hard to forget. I was employed by the

BBC to act as an expert advising contestants in a game show as to what items they should buy at an antiques fair to sell at an auction later and make a profit.

'Didn't we laugh, it only sold for a tenner!'

The man was obviously a big fan of the programme, as he went on to recount the numerous times I had failed miserably in my role as expert. He knew more about the show than I did. I didn't want to appear rude by cutting him short but I simply wanted to get on my way. I walked purposefully round to the rear of the car and suggested we should perhaps make a start. At last, I thought, as he followed me. He whistled, wandered back to his van and returned with an enormous wheel-brace in his hand. Progress was being made, or at least I thought so, then he stopped.

'What about that 1950s plastic cinema figure of a girl in a swimsuit you told 'em to buy? Turned out it was brand-new and they lost a packet. We laughed at that as well.'

This man was a walking encyclopaedia of Serrell television faux-pas. I didn't feel I could interrupt and it took nearly two and a half hours to change my tyre as he regaled me with stories of my bloomers.

By the time I eventually arrived home I was totally exhausted and ready for bed, consoled by the thought that at least I had got the birds to sell.

The sale for the Dorothy Doughty lots was about three weeks away and with the library descriptions and photographs to hand the catalogue entries were ready in minutes. It was time to trawl through my little black book and unearth some customers who might wish to add the birds to their collections. I identified about ten and made sure that the girls in the office had got them on the mailing register for the sale catalogues. I thought I had better phone Don to find out when the kitchen delivery man would drop the birds off at the saleroom.

'Eer, 'e was coming down next week to do that job in the Midlands but the lady's not gonner be there for another ten days so I'll give you a call then.'

That was all right, provided they were with us before the catalogues went to press. It was a quick turnaround time with the printers and it might just be cutting it a bit fine. Don, in his cheery manner, assured me there was no need to worry. Give me nothing to worry about and I'll worry about having nothing to worry about. Still, I was really in their hands.

Ten days later I had heard nothing from Don; it was time to make another phone call.

''E'll be down on the ninth, no worries – I'm a man of me werd.'

There was nothing I could do except trust

in Don; the ninth was the day before the view day and really was the eleventh hour. The catalogues went out on the appointed day with the birds fully illustrated and the telephones started to ring, including three calls from some of the customers I had earmarked. They all indicated their wish to come to the sale. That was very pleasing and I was beginning to feel quietly confident.

The week before a sale is normally hectic with all manner of enquiries to be answered and I had put the arrival of the kitchen delivery man to the back of my mind, when, on the ninth at about ten thirty, he arrived in the saleroom. Don was as good as his word.

'Eer, I've got Don's beards in the van. Where d'you wan' 'em?'

Relief. All was now well and I could rest easy.

'Just bring them in, please; put them on the table and we can unpack them.'

'Sound, mate.'

In they came. I should have realised something was amiss when the boxes he carried in were not the large, pre-formed, polystyrene originals provided by the Royal Worcester porcelain factory, but were simply orange boxes. Not only that but the packing materials were not the expanded foam and bubble wrap that we would have used, but week-old, coffee-stained newspapers.

Slowly I delved into each box, insisting that the kitchen delivery man stood next to me to witness what was to emerge. Every piece was broken beyond all recognition. The limited editions for each model had now been reduced by one. I didn't know what to say; I just knew I had to phone Don straight away.

'Don, it's Philip here; the birds have arrived. I'm not really sure there's an easy way to tell you this but each one is smashed to bits.'

I waited for him to explode as I know I would have done. He seemed strangely calm and then said, 'At least we've got 'em insured at the original valuations.'

No, he wouldn't have done that, surely not a pre-planned insurance claim (would he?).

Lot 14

Maude Hart, R.I.P.

'Philip, Maude Hart has been rushed into hospital and things don't look good.'

The telephone call came from a London-based accountant who looked after the affairs of one Maude Hart.

Part of the way auctioneers made their

living was from clearing houses either when clients were unable to cope and had to move into a nursing home or, in worst-case scenarios, where a death had occurred. One's emotions at such a time are mixed: sadness for the family and friends, but also joy at the prospect of good things to sell. The latter always arouses guilt, particularly if you know the person involved, but I rationalise this by taking the view that if you didn't do the job someone else would. I'm sure undertakers must feel the same.

The accountant told me that Mrs Hart had collapsed in her home and was due to undergo emergency surgery. She had been a client of the firm for a long time and I had met her on several occasions with Mr Rayer, who acted as the family's agent looking after the various properties they had acquired through the years. This primarily involved collecting rents and seeking new tenants as they became vacant. Mrs Hart was a small, wiry lady aged about eighty with a shock of white hair. What was particularly striking about her was her general appearance: she was always immaculate in timeless and no doubt expensive clothes. Yet the cost of her wardrobe was not a display of wealth, as she was of the opinion that if you bought the best it always lasted. Her clothes were never discarded due to fashion but only out of necessity. Whenever I visited her home I found her very precise with her instructions: she certainly could not be classified as a 'pushover little old lady'. Any unwanted door-to-door salesman was soon dismissed with a sharp word from Mrs Hart.

The family used to live in a large Regency house in one of Worcester's best residential squares. Mrs Hart had no living relatives. She had married during the Second World War and, apparently, adored her husband, who was killed in action; something she had never got over. Her ancestors were wealthy and their prudence had created a capital sum that provided an income that far exceeded her needs. She was a careful lady who realised that the old family home was too big and had downsized before such a word ever became fashionable.

After the telephone call from her accountant I found myself driving to her home, which was a large 1960s detached house on the outskirts of the city. It was, like her, immaculate but although it had been fastidiously maintained, it had not been updated in any way. The kitchen had the same type of units as Fanny Craddock had in those old black and white television cookery programmes. The lampshades were very 1960 – ironically nowadays very sought after – and the floors throughout the house were covered in dated, patterned carpets.

Maude Hart had never bought an antique

in her life. She hadn't needed to: she was surrounded by the stuff. Her forefathers must have had the same thrifty view of life as she had. The family furniture had been bought between roughly 1780 and 1880 and, as it had always been looked after, had never been replaced. She was always proud of her home and appreciated the lovely things that surrounded her; everywhere you looked were choice items that would raise the heart rate of any collector. The furniture was predominantly late Georgian oak and mahogany complemented by silver, brass, porcelain and paintings of the same period.

The accountant had followed his initial remark on the telephone with, 'It looks like everything will have to be sold but in the short term we would like your advice with regard to security at the house.'

My sense of sadness at Maude Hart's current state was, I am ashamed to say, more than compensated for by the thought that I was probably going to be instructed to sell the contents of her home. I arrived at the front door, keys in hand, and slowly opened the plain white-painted door with its dated bull's-eye glass in the centre. There was no burglar alarm installed, which was worrying. This was my chance to have a closer look at the lovely things that had been in the Hart family, in some cases, since they were bought new. There was a longcase clock – the auctioneer's term for a grandfather clock – and a handsome oak side table covered in highly polished brass and copper. It was not just the furniture that glowed with patina – the rich colour that comes with age – but metalware as well. The brass candlesticks were early eighteenth century and had a full, mellow colour that almost talked, so deep was their glow. Prints of old Worcester showing sailing barges on the River Severn behind the racecourse and various prospects of the city hung from the walls.

The dining room was dominated by a huge oak dresser with cupboards and a delft rack. A dresser is rather like a sideboard that normally has three drawers and is raised on legs, but in this instance the gap between the drawers and the floor was filled in with cupboards. The delft rack over was an arrangement of shelves that were originally intended to display the early eighteenth-century blue and white wares (known as delft) that came originally not only from Holland, but were also made in London, Liverpool and Bristol. These dressers are normally about six or seven feet wide but this monster was at least ten feet from side to side.

A pair of paintings in the drawing room drew the eye. They were, I guessed, from about 1820 and were finely painted still-life studies of flowers and insects. I had always wondered who they were by but a close inspection revealed no signature; there was still no doubting the quality. These would need the expert eye of the man known to all of us in the saleroom as the 'Picture Man' cast over them. In the trade he was well known for having a marvellous eye and phenomenal knowledge.

These few pieces were but a sample from a houseful that auctioneers dream about. Most of them hadn't been moved, other than to be cleaned, since being thoughtfully positioned when Mrs Hart had moved into her new-built home about thirty-five years ago.

A total lack of any security measures rendered this an extremely vulnerable house. The neighbours kindly looked after the property as best they could but the situation was not very satisfactory. News travels fast and I was concerned that the availability of rich pickings would attract any budding burglar. I rang the accountant from my mobile telephone.

'Philip, Maude has worsened if anything and is not expected to make the night. Could you arrange to clear the house of the valuables first thing in the morning? Store them initially, but the way it looks, you may as well catalogue it all for your next sale.'

I was beginning to feel guilty as I relished the thought of dealing with this treasure trove of a houseful – while Mrs Hart lay seriously ill in hospital. The next call was to our removal man, Nigel Hodges, a terrific lad, aged about thirty-five, built like a brick outhouse, who went by the imaginative name of 'Big Nige'. His strength was phenomenal; when a piano had to be delivered to the saleroom he seemed to appear with it tucked under his arm. He was about six feet four inches tall and must have weighed a very solid eighteen stone. His appetite was legendary and if he came into the saleroom around lunchtime he would, more often than not, be accompanied by four huge doorstep sausage sandwiches, lashed with brown sauce, as he called out his familiar cheery, 'Hi-de-Hi.' Nothing was ever too much trouble and every request was met with the response, 'Can do,' and then an unfussed accomplishment of the task, followed by an equally cheery, 'Bysey-Bye.' Even more noticeable than Big Nige's sheer bulk was his attempt at corporate uniform. This was a violent, electric-blue polo shirt adorned with brilliant white embroidery depicting a removal van with 'HODGE'S HANTIQUE HAULAGE' in bold three-inch-high script above it. Subtle it was not, but he was proud of his logo which had taken some months of thought and planning on his part.

An auctioneer places a great deal of trust in his removal man and Nigel never let me down. There were, no doubt, opportunities for him to help himself to a hidden snippet while clearing a house, but Big Nige wouldn't have known how to deviate from 100 per cent honesty. The only thing we ever fell out over was his constant whistling of naff 1980s pop tunes. That they were naff wasn't the major problem, it was the fact that Nigel managed to attain a key that wasn't in the original score, and certainly did nothing to improve on the original. He was one of the few people I knew who could whistle, unwittingly, in tune to Les Dawson's piano playing.

Like all hauliers he had an assistant. Eric was about sixty and smoked like a chimney. He was an ardent shopper at charity shops – an admirable habit, as you can help others while picking up bargains. Eric, however, chose clothes that at best could be described as loose fitting. They always seemed at least three sizes too big. He also had a penchant for 'Frank Spencer pullovers' and huge check trousers. The whole ensemble was set off by his eyewear. He was forever losing glasses and so had to look for cheap sources. He had found a shop that sold second-hand prescription spectacles. His method of choosing a pair was to take the classified section of the local newspaper with him, hold it about eighteen inches from his eyes and try to read it with the chosen pair of glasses. This method, though surely not recommended, seemed to work for him – except in one respect. Eric was not a slave to fashion and once he had found a pair that passed the test he was happy, and blithely unconcerned as to who the original owner had been. It was always a joy when he came into the saleroom, for you never knew what style of spectacles he'd be wearing. The only certainty was that they would look completely ridiculous, ranging from severe Harry Potter look-alikes to flamboyant Dame Edna Everage specials.

Big Nige was able to help and could be there in the morning at eight thirty sharp. Well, there was nothing to be done that night so I carefully relocked the house and set off for home.

I arrived at the house in the morning and was so engrossed in further exploring the contents of Maude Hart's home that I didn't hear the footsteps until the familiar greeting followed. 'Hi-de-Hi' Big Nige had arrived and two paces behind, like a faithful old Labrador, was Eric. Proudly he showed me his new charity shop purchase: thick black-rimmed glasses with pitch-black lenses. He looked like Roy Orbison going to a bad taste party. I gave them their instructions and set about making a list of the more valuable items in the house that we needed to move to the saleroom. In effect this was almost everything there. I thought we would have finished by lunchtime but it was late afternoon before the last piece was safely packed in the van. I rang the accountant to tell him that our task was completed and the contents were now safe from burglary. I felt awful as I realised that I had almost forgotten about poor Maude Hart and, almost as an afterthought, enquired if there was any further news, expecting the worst.

'I don't know how, but she made the op; the doctors don't hold out too much hope. You may as well get on with the cataloguing.'

Big Nige was going to drop everything off at the saleroom so that we could begin the task of cataloguing the contents prior to getting the catalogue printed. It took about four days to go through the almost 300 lots: they would constitute a sale in their own right. By luck the Picture Man called in to the saleroom while we were going through the lots. Nervously I showed him the pair of paintings that I so much admired. When had his response ever matched up to my enthusiasm?

'Not bad, ought to do eight to twelve.'

'Eight to twelve what?' I countered.

'Thousand; they're probably French, late eighteenth or early nineteenth century,' he replied as he walked out through the door of the saleroom. He was on his way to another auction sale where he had spotted a modern painting which he thought was worth £3,000 to £4,000. The auctioneers did not have the services of a Picture Man to call on and they hadn't recognised it. What's more, he didn't think anyone else had spotted it.

It was time to contact the accountant and tell him that the cataloguing was completed and we were now ready to enter the lots into a sale.

'Excellent, Philip. I'm pleased that you managed to get it all out of the house so quickly. As a matter of course you had better let me know when the auction is going to be.'

I tentatively asked how his client was.

'Really not very good; it's a sad job but it is something that will come to us all one day.'

There was little I could do for Mrs Hart but I wanted to do the best I could for her with the antiques that we had catalogued. It was now a matter of deciding which lots we should illustrate, the choice being vast. Eventually we decided the two star lots that we would put on the cover of the catalogue would be the pair of paintings and the huge dresser. The paintings presented no problem to photograph as they were so small and portable; the dresser however was a different matter. Big Nige had originally moved it out of the house to his van on a device called a piano trolley. This was like a low four-wheeled go-kart, or buggy, which slid under a piano so it could be wheeled around easily with a person at each end. To photograph the dresser we needed natural light; this meant we had to move this huge piece of furniture outside the saleroom. Said quickly thus – a simple task. But the entrance to the saleroom was by way of two huge stone steps, which presented the first problem. When it was delivered I had been engrossed in doing something else; quite how they had managed to bring it through the doors I didn't know.

'Right, let's each take an end,' Big Nige instructed. I had to feel sorry for Eric. When moving a heavy object down a set of stairs all the weight is at the end that goes down first, and that's where poor Eric was, while Big Nige and I were at the easy end. His Roy Orbison glasses misted up and his face went every shade of red before settling on a deep magenta colour. The dresser, which was still on the piano trolley, lurched down the steps frighteningly quickly. Suddenly it was totally out of control. Eric, valiantly and perhaps a little foolhardily, was not about to desert his post, which I'm afraid to say I had now done. He had clambered aboard the dresser and was hanging on for dear life as it shot down the drive towards the road. By now the girls in the office had come out to watch and we all stared helplessly as Eric gathered momentum like an out-of-control bobsleigh careering down the Cresta Run.

"'Elp, 'elp,' came the pitiful cries from Eric.

I couldn't see that we had any hope of stopping it but my major concern was what would happen when Eric and the dresser shot out of the saleroom gate and careered into the main road. Then my worries disappeared. Big Nige leaped into action. He took off with surprising speed for such a big man, grabbed a block of wood and threw it under the wheels of the trolley. The whole episode was rather like an old Buster Keaton film where they were trying to stop the runaway train trolley that had the pretty heroine strapped to it; except that Eric was neither pretty nor a heroine. The dresser stopped just as quickly as in the film. The same could not be said for Eric. He shot off the end of the dresser airborne like a trapeze artist. I am ashamed to say that I was concentrating on the dresser – thank God it was unharmed. Eric looked as if the biggest wound was going to be to his pride as he landed in a very prickly bush just inside the gate to the saleroom. The photographs eventually came out wonderfully well, which is more than can be said for Eric's derrière.

A few days passed and other matters surpassed the Hart question; that is until her accountant telephoned the saleroom.

'Philip, she's still with us. It's a bit touch and go but she's confounded all the medics.'

Apparently Mrs Hart, with the tenacity and fighting spirit that she had exhibited all her life, was refusing to answer the call from above.

'She's certainly not going home even if she does pull through this – and that's a big if. Let me have a schedule of your recommended reserves for the sale but I'm afraid I can't give you final instructions at the moment.'

We managed to put together a list of reserves and posted it on to the accountant; all we could do now was wait for the decision to go ahead with the sale. It was exciting looking forward to the auction but the uncertainty over the exact sale date was a little off-putting; most auctioneers like to get the goods in and sell them as soon as possible – it's part of the ongoing cycle. Several more days passed before the accountant rang again.

'Philip, old Maude has confounded them all – Lord knows how – and she looks like she might make it. She's now able to talk reasonably coherently and they're going to break it to her that she is going to have to go into a home.'

While I was keen to sell the contents of Mrs Hart's house I really felt for her at the prospect of moving into a home and losing most of the possessions that had been such an important part of her life for so long – particularly as she was always so proud that her antiques had been in the family for generations.

Several weeks had now passed by and I did not have the time to give a lot of thought to the Hart sale. The saleroom was busy in other respects, as it always was, and although I wanted to get on with the job, there seemed little point in fretting about circumstances that were so clearly out of my control. Then came another telephone call from the accountant.

'Philip, Maude is going home. She's amazed the doctors, but if she carries on improving at the rate she has she should be ready to leave in about three weeks.'

My immediate reaction was twofold: 'Good old Maude!' and, 'Damn me, there goes my sale.' I was obviously delighted that she had made such a marvellous recovery, but I could not deny the twinge of disappointment that my star sale had disappeared in a telephone call.

The next three weeks passed in a whirl of activity even more frenzied than ever. Her accountant was taking charge of preparing the house in readiness for her return and I was to ensure that everything was replaced just how it was before she was rushed into hospital. I've cleared many houses in my career but this was the first time that everything had to be put back. Eventually it was all in its rightful place for the day of her homecoming, looking just as it had before we had removed it from the house. I was pleased with the results.

Some two months later I had a message in the office to telephone Mrs Hart. I duly did and was delighted to be invited to go round and have tea with her one afternoon. The day arrived and I presented myself at her front door and was ushered into the drawing room. We spent an hour or so talking about her treasured possessions, for she was a knowledgeable lady, and enjoyed debating the relative merits of her collection. Then, a little tongue in cheek, she said, 'You did a marvellous job getting everything back where it was, but you know those two little paintings on the wall over there?' She pointed to the two still-life studies praised by the Picture Man. 'Well, you've hung them the wrong way around.'

Good old Maude, I chuckled to myself.

Two years passed before we had another telephone call from her accountant.

'Philip, Mrs Hart has been rushed into hospital.'

This time Maude didn't pull through and died within the week. It was rather upsetting clearing the house for a second time, yet in a strange way I felt she was watching over my every move, particularly when I took the two small paintings off the wall.

The draft catalogues and photographs were dug out from two years previously and this time her lots actually made the auction. The saleroom was packed with buyers all competing to own a small part of Maude Hart's home. Most of the locals had either known her or known of her and the prices far and away exceeded my estimates. The pair of paintings sold for £10,000 – the Picture Man was always spot-on with his estimates – and the dresser made £5,000. I was pleased with the sale but felt a little sad that my home city had lost another of its characters.

Lot 15

'Only a Sketch, But Good'

'Bugger off!'

That was not the response I was expecting. I waited a few moments and knocked on the door again. Same answer.

'Bugger off!'

I was standing outside the door of Skelton Manor, the country home of Sir Nimrod Langwill, Bart, and this was not what I expected to hear from a titled gentleman. Skelton Manor was a huge red brick house dating back to the William and Mary period of about 1690. Its most striking features were the tall spiralling chimney stacks which stood out like beacons. The manor was not in pristine order; it was a home that was most definitely lived in and, as in many cases, its owners had not necessarily kept their maintenance programme bang up to date. In the case of Skelton this was not down to a lack of funds but simply that the current, and the preceding, baronets had not got around to putting in hand the various jobs required. 'Nimmy', as he liked to be called, was the son of an old client of Mr Rayer and lived in the huge pile that was approached by a mile-long tarmacadam driveway that wound its way up a gently sloping hill in the heart of the Shropshire countryside. The house itself sat in a wooded bowl on the top of a hill that could not be seen from the B road from which its drive turned off. It was some two years since I had last been to Skelton; about the time that Nimmy took over the estate when his father had died. The new baronet worked in Whitehall and was something to do with the nation's security, which I always found a little worrying, since he was a rather eccentric and scatty character. I knocked for a third time.

'Bugger off!'

Something didn't sound quite right with

the voice and this time I was sure I heard a muffled chortle emanating from behind the front door. Slowly there was a creak as the huge piece of ancient timber opened on its massive wrought-iron hinges. There was Nimmy, hardly able to contain himself, doubled up with laughter. He was dressed not unlike Bertie Wooster in wide grey flannel trousers, highly polished brogues and his old Oxford college cricket sweater. The latter looked slightly incongruous, it being some thirty-odd years old, somewhat moth-eaten and under some pressure as Nimmy had added a few pounds to his frame since his university days. In his hand I noticed a bag, containing what looked like bird seed, and there appeared to be pink and yellow feathers on the deep red Turkish carpet laid over the huge flagstones of the hall floor.

'Look!' he said, pointing to a bird cage hidden behind the front door. 'I've called her Margaret in honour of Mrs T.'

You did not have to be a genius to work out Nimmy's political allegiance. Margaret was a parrot.

'I'm teaching her to talk and I thought it would be a real whizz if I could train her to say, "Bugger off!" whenever anyone knocked on the front door.'

That was typical of Nimmy; life was very much to be enjoyed, and nothing fazed him. At the time of my last visit, in the depths of winter, the whole heating system in the house had packed up, dry rot had been discovered in the cellars, and there were holes in the roof that a flock of ostriches, let alone pigeons, could have got through. Nimmy's response to this was to pop into Ludlow and try to buy some ice skates as he thought the duck pond, which was frozen over, would probably be load-bearing.

'D'you know I haven't skated since I was twelve in that really bad winter of 1963.'

This summed up his attitude to life; or at least the part of it I witnessed. He went on to explain the reason for my current visit.

'This place is a bit of a project' – that was the biggest understatement since Noah said it looked like rain – 'and having sorted the cellar I thought it was time to have a look at the roof. There's a lot of tat up there and I was rather hoping you might be able to sell some of it at your place. At the moment you can't really see the wood for the trees up there. I thought I might make some headway if I created some space so the contractors can actually have a look and see what needs doing.'

'Look at the roof.' I would have thought it was easier to look through the roof rather than at it. This, however, was really exciting as old country houses such as this one tend to have goodies tucked away that haven't seen the light of day for many years, and hopefully there could be a hidden nugget that would be the star lot in one of my sales.

'Would you mind awfully having a look for me?'

I didn't need a second invitation and off we went up the great staircase with its ornate iron balustrade. As we walked up we were followed by the eyes of Nimmy's ancestors, which peered out from the portrait paintings that lined the walls. I had always been fascinated by the family history of private homes like this one, and although Nimmy was not a man to brag about his good fortune, he took simple pride and delight in telling me that he could trace his family history back to about 1080 and that for most of that time his family had lived in Shropshire. It made me feel somewhat inadequate as my family history was only traceable to about 1870.

I remembered being in the library on a previous visit with Mr Rayer, marvelling at the yards of books detailing the family's connections with the county. Among them, estate books with old ledgers recorded its management during the nineteenth century, detailing how important the manor and surrounding land were to the village and villagers of Skelton. The joy of Nimmy was that he was so keen to share all this history, regarding himself simply as its curator, preserving it for the next generation. This in itself was slightly bizarre, because as far as I could see, there was no Lady Langwill, Nimmy being a confirmed bachelor, and I had no idea who was heir to this glorious piece of old England.

On we walked, the stairs becoming slightly less grand as we made our way up to the second floor, originally the servants' quarters. All the doors to the various rooms were now closed, but part of the fun of a visit like this was to imagine what lay behind them. We continued our climb up another flight of stairs to the attic rooms. To put the rooms into context, each one's floor area was probably greater than that of the whole of most modern houses. Again the doors were shut but this time their secret contents were about to be revealed. Would it be Chippendale or Sheraton, Constable or Gainsborough? It might be something obscure that I knew nothing about; my excitement was tinged with a little anxiety.

'I hope I'm not wasting your time; it really is a great help you coming over like this. I am obviously willing to pay your fee if everything in here really is rubbish.' My titled friend was clearly feeling a little embarrassed at the prospect that I might be on a fool's errand. There was no need for him to worry; I was happy just to share the day with such a delightful character and drink in the atmosphere of this wonderful old house.

'You know the trouble with the Langwills is that, while we have always appreciated living here, we perhaps haven't paid as much attention to everyday repairs as we should. I think the family motto is never do today what you can put off until tomorrow.'

I told Nimmy that in my experience most families were like that, tending to ignore what was under their noses. I think the expression is that familiarity breeds contempt.

'Very kind of you, old boy, but we have been a little tardy. This place is like the Forth Bridge: it needs constant painting. Trouble is, the Langwill tribe never got the paint can out in the first place, as it were, and now it's all up to me.'

I was desperate for Nimmy to open the door so that we could see what the attics held. He stood there wistfully, hand on the door knob, seemingly gazing into the past. Eventually the door opened and I was taken aback, not by the contents, but because I had been expecting a damp, musty room with little light and lots of cobwebs. I had forgotten the holes in the roof. The sunlight shone through the cavernous voids which had ensured excellent ventilation, no doubt gales in bad weather, but, surprisingly, hardly any obvious rain damage. Although this had not given the spiders a chance to spin their webs, it had given the pigeons opportunity to leave some fairly substantial deposits. Disappointingly, the room did not appear to hold any great hidden treasure. There was a reason for secreting things in the attic in the first place, of course: they simply weren't good enough to keep in the lower floors. Thinking about it, I should have realised that we all put our unwanted clutter in the attic.

However, it looked saleable stuff, though most of it would be put through our general collectables sales. There were marble-top tile-back washstands, wash jug and bowl sets, broken folding screens, and boxes and boxes of old glass and other clutter that had built up over many years. Interestingly there was also a signed photograph of Winston Churchill, somewhat tarnished by a disrespectful pigeon; the family's political ties seemed to be fairly long-standing. The bulk of the 'atticus rubbishus', as Nimmy described it, had come from the lesser servants' quarters. Never mind, there were still two other large rooms to look in: perhaps all was not lost.

The second room was very much the same story, although I imagined its contents came from the rooms of the higher-ranking members of the household staff. Here there were pine chests of drawers that dated from the Regency period of about 1820. Fortunately these pieces had not been stripped back to the timber as was the fashion in the late 1980s, but retained the original paint that would have decorated them all those years ago. They were likely to fetch between £300 and £500 each at auction. Unlike the previous room, this one mainly contained furniture, with very little by way of smaller items hidden away in boxes. One room to go: perhaps this would be the winner. Before opening the door Nimmy paused again.

'You know we really need to clear this lot so the old place can have a bit of love and care.' At last Nimmy opened the door to the third room.

Nothing. Well, that was not strictly true as it seemed that the world's supply of wooden towel rails dating back to about 1890 had been stacked in this room. There were rails of every description and timber; some painted, some carved and some relying solely on design for their appeal. Regrettably most of them were damaged or broken, the whole now resembling a three-dimensional jigsaw of interwoven sticks of wood. Most were more suitable for the fire than the saleroom, but some were salvagcable. I supposed that they must have been discarded up here when the house had central heating installed.

Hey-ho! No world beaters that I could see but it had been a lovely day out, excellent company and a glorious drive through the countryside of Worcestershire and Shropshire. We made our way back down the various staircases to the ground floor and to Nimmy's office where we looked at our diaries to arrange a suitable date for the attic contents to be delivered to the sale-room. I sat down, grateful to accept a cup of coffee from the latest gadget that my host had bought. He was a sucker for the newest contraption sold in the fashionable London shops, the crazes often being short-lived. It was an all-singing, all-dancing espresso-type machine that produced the frothy, foaming brews that the trendy café bars now sold. It brought a wry smile to my face to think that in another hundred years' time this contraption could well find its way into the attic and be discussed by my and Nimmy's successors as to what this strange appliance was originally used for, its saleability and value.

I glanced across the clutter that filled the office and noticed a small painting leaning up against his desk.

'What's the little picture, Nimmy?' I asked.

'Forgotten that – glad you spotted it. I found it in a box in the first attic among the things I wanted to sell. I broke the frame when I dropped a box on it, so brought it down here meaning to fix it and the truth is I clean forgot about it.'

Well, I couldn't claim to be a paintings

expert; in fact I'm not sure I could claim to be an expert in anything, but this little picture, an oil painting, certainly looked as though it had some potential. It was filthy dirty with the inevitable pigeon deposits, but I could just distinguish what I thought looked like either a cow or a horse. It would be worth getting the Picture Man to take a closer look at it. I told Nimmy that I would take the picture back with me in my car, but that I was a little concerned about transport costs for the rest of the contents of the attics. If we had to pay hauliers to bring it into the saleroom there would most likely be the middle and both ends of nothing left for my genial host after we had sold everything. I voiced my concern and, ever cheerful, back came the response.

'No problem, old chap, this is a job that dear old Maurice and I can tackle.'

Maurice, I assumed, was an old family retainer pressed into service when a job like this came about. He was going to love me – an endless quantity of country house cast-offs to carry down three huge flights of stairs.

Making my way back to the saleroom, I pulled up along one particular lane near Malvern that I had always found enchanting. It was home to an old farmer who I had no doubt would have met my old boss in some way or another around the county. He would

213

have been about eighty then and had since moved into this bungalow. His front garden was an absolute picture, adorned with geraniums and fuchsias without a weed in sight. However, his real pride and joy was in the field next to his home: his two closest companions, two huge Shire horses that used to work the land many years ago. I would often see him leaning on the gate talking to them. They were all growing old together, and you could see the affectionate bond that existed between the three of them. I found these creatures captivating; astonishing power combined with extraordinary grace, a living definition of the term 'work-horse'. Seeing them reminded me of Nimmy's painting; I was sure I could see an outline of a horse in the middle of the canvas. But I had little time to stop and think: I had to get back to the saleroom. I had lots of work to do, including clearing some space to store the rest of Nimmy's items which were due in a couple of days. Besides, the Picture Man wouldn't be in before the end of the week.

It was one of those very busy times and the days fled by; the imminent arrival of the Skelton Manor consignment completely slipped my mind. It was official coffee time, about eleven o'clock (as opposed to unofficial coffee time, the difference being that the official one was accompanied by biscuits), when the door to the office swung open and in walked Nimmy.

'Morning, chaps, any chance of a coffee? You really ought to get one of those machines like mine – damn good tools. Those biscuits look good too; don't suppose there's a jammy dodger left?'

We quietly put the world to rights over the next few minutes, almost forgetting the purpose of his visit. There were now no jammy dodgers left in the biscuit tin.

'We'd better go and sort Maurice out,' said our friendly baronet, rising and striding towards the door.

I was quite looking forward to meeting Maurice but I felt hugely embarrassed that I hadn't asked him in for coffee and a biscuit. Then I reasoned that probably domestic staff would be trained to wait outside; I was sure he could tell a tale or two about his boss. I expected to see a grey-haired old man, perhaps with a slight stoop, dutifully standing beside a loaded vehicle but I was wrong. Maurice was Morris the vehicle itself, Nimmy's treasured grey 1952 Morris Motors lorry, which his father had bought new for the estate, and which had remained there ever since.

'You've got to be a wealthy man to drive one of these, Philip.'

'Why's that, Nimmy – is it worth a lot?' I asked, still slightly bemused and feeling rather foolish.

'No,' came back the reply, 'it's petrol not diesel and only does about eight miles to the gallon.'

As we began unloading Morris, the stuff seemed worse rather than better than I remembered; the surroundings of a house like Skelton Manor must have given me rose-tinted spectacles. Almost all the furniture was either broken or damaged in some way or other, and the boxes of smalls, the term for non-furniture items in a sale, now looked decidedly average. My hopes of a host of entries for my next fine art and antique sale evaporated in front of my eyes. Nimmy didn't seem too concerned with what happened to the 'atticus rubbishus'. Still, there was always the painting. We eventually finished unloading Morris and Nimmy drove off in a cloud of smoke with a cheery wave.

At the end of the week the Picture Man came into the saleroom. He could spot an important sixteenth-century Old Master just as easily as a piece of twentieth-century Modernism. The Picture Man had only three expressions for lots he looked at for me: 'Rubbish', 'Not bad' and 'Pretty good'. In the past, everything I had shown him had generated one of the first two responses, nothing I had had in the saleroom being good enough to warrant a 'Pretty good'. Having initially built up my hopes with regard to the little painting with the broken frame I was now having doubts. Rather nervously I went to the paintings rack and came back with Nimmy's 'smudger' (a slang term in the trade for a painting) and hesitantly handed it to him.

'That's good!'

I was quite taken aback; acclaim of this magnitude was unheard of, this was off the Richter scale of praise.

The Picture Man was close to being enthusiastic, even excited. There was still one question to ask: 'How much do you think it might make?'

'Fifty, might do seventy,' he enlightened me.

'Oh,' I mumbled. The whole episode seemed like a bizarre daydream; I was about to ask if he was sure and meant thousands when he spoke again.

'Stubbs, George Stubbs, small and only a sketch, but good.'

I was knocked back sideways. Stubbs was an eighteenth-century English artist who specialised in horse subjects. He was one of the most important artists of his type and for the last two to three weeks I had been walking past one of his works in my saleroom.

'Good thing this,' he continued. 'I should estimate it at between fifty and eighty thousand. Anything else to look at? I've got another sale to go and view.'

Well, he was all very matter-of-fact, but then he dealt with things like this on an almost daily basis. I told him there was nothing else. I was still rather dumbfounded by the rave review he had given the little horse picture.

As soon as the Picture Man left I telephoned Nimmy to tell him the good news. He did not appear to be in any way as excited as I was; indeed he was decidedly distracted. I was concerned that he might decide not to sell the Stubbs after all. After some gentle probing I eventually got to the reason for his seeming lack of interest. Morris had failed its MOT, and he was really worried about the future for his lifelong friend. Morris was a lot closer to Nimmy's heart than the painting. But my concerns were soon alleviated as he confirmed his instructions for me to go ahead and sell it. I suggested we place a reserve, or minimum selling price, on it of £50,000. He agreed, but still wasn't paying much attention, being more concerned with Morris's sticking piston rings and rusting chassis. This, no doubt, accounted for the cloud of smoke it had emitted on leaving the sale-room a few days back.

Each vendor is different and while this amount of money might seem like a lottery win to most, it obviously wasn't leaping to the forefront of Nimmy's preoccupied mind. I did manage to extract from him that the Stubbs had been at Skelton for as long as he could remember but other than that he knew nothing about it.

I decided to include the painting in my next fine art sale and really go to town with the pre-sale promotional publicity. I intended to advertise it extensively, not only in our usual auction advert but also to take out a special half-page advert in the trade paper, with a large photograph of the painting on its own and the date of the auction. I also wanted the girls in the office to trawl through all the trade directories so that we could direct-mail our catalogues to all the dealers and collectors who might be interested. There was to be no stone left un-turned in the marketing of the Stubbs. Letters with photographs would be sent out to anyone with even the remotest interest in buying the painting.

In the meantime there were the rest of the Skelton Manor lots to sort through. All the boxes of smalls were unpacked. It soon became apparent that there was very little to get excited about: lots of glassware, old silver and other odds and ends including, ironically, an early example of a coffee-making machine that Nimmy's father had discarded some years ago. It was clearly a hereditary thing. Our task was to group the goods into lots that would prove attractive to the bidders, then put the items forming a lot back into the boxes under the tables in the saleroom with the occasional better bits lotted separately on the tabletop. This was duly done and we were ready for the next general sale the following week. The Stubbs auction was later in the month and I had plenty of work to do in the meantime to ensure a successful day.

Photographs were important and I was happy with the images we had taken of the picture. Genuine articles that are un-restored or touched in any way, in my experience, always sell better and I decided that we should leave the Stubbs just as it was found. The photographer had managed, despite the guano, almost to improve on the real thing. It would obviously take pride of place on the front cover of the catalogue. I began to contact the main dealers to tell them that the painting was coming up for auction. I was really excited by the prospect of the sale but the reaction from the dealers did seem somewhat subdued. I reasoned that these top dealers handle lots like this all the time and it was no big deal for them; for a Stubbs, it was at the lower end of the market. A full-size Stubbs with provenance would possibly make between £500,000 and £1 million. I also reassured myself that they would be wary of showing their hand too soon. The adverts were placed, proofs were approved and I was pleased with the way the catalogue itself was looking. I was confident of a good result.

There is a never-ending cycle within salerooms: we are always just having had a sale, having a sale, or getting ready for the next sale. Thoughts of the Stubbs had to take a back seat as the following day was the view day for the general sale in which the rest of the Skelton Manor lots were included. Some people only attend general sales because they perceive them to be at their level of interest; the same goes for the fine art sales. Naturally there is some crossover between the two types but each sale definitely has its own character – and also its own characters. The dealers at the lesser sales, by and large, sell their wares to larger dealers, either directly, or through small shops, flea markets, car-boot sales and collectors' fairs. I never cease to be amazed by the diverse range of buyers and the equally wide range of items they will buy.

The bulk of the furniture buyers were shipping dealers. They predominantly bought late Victorian and 1920s furniture that was shipped in containers to America and elsewhere; hence the term. They would not, however, pass up the opportunity to bid on any good lot when they had the chance. They travelled miles, worked long hours six days a week and traded on small profits and huge volumes of turnover. They also had mastered the art of loading or, rather, over-loading their cars, typically Volvo estates. I have seen them leave my saleroom with as many bedroom suites tied on board as you would have loaded on a five-ton lorry. Hopefully the demand for pine chests of drawers and broken towel rails would be pretty strong at the moment in the USA and the Skelton Manor lots would do well.

The buyers of the smalls were also a likeable bunch, hoovering up vast quantities of china, glass, silver plate and the like for a seemingly insatiable market. The current craze for kitchenalia might even see the prototype coffee machine find a new home.

The sale went as well as I'd hoped: the pine chests realised between £380 and £720 and the boxes of smalls generally exceeded expectations. Even the coffee machine sold for £18, probably more than it had cost new. In all, the Skelton Manor consignment came to nearly £7,000.

I telephoned Nimmy the next day to give him the sale results. He was really pleased; although not so much with the sale results, rather that Morris was apparently not now destined for the big garage in the sky. Its piston rings and chassis were in the process of being sorted. All was again well in the world of Sir Nimrod Langwill, Bart.

'Sorry, dear boy, almost forgot, delighted

with the sale results, seven grand for all that. Good Lord, I could buy a friend for Morris!'

Well, he seemed pleased; I just hoped there was even better news to come with the Stubbs.

The next day I was on the phone to all the dealers, again making sure that they had received their catalogues. The adverts had started to appear but the telephone was certainly quieter than I had expected. Obviously, I thought, all the major dealers were sure to make the journey up from London to view the painting in situ, and not rely upon the digital images we sent out.

View day duly arrived for what became affectionately known by us as the 'Nimmy Piccie' sale. 'Lot 124: George Stubbs – oil on canvas – Sketch Study of a Bay horse in an open landscape. 8ins x 12ins. Provenance: From Skelton Manor, the home of Sir Nimrod Langwill, Bart.' I had huge hopes and expectation riding on these three lines of the catalogue.

After about three hours' viewing one of the major dealers of this type of painting walked into the room – all those phone calls, letters, photographs and catalogues had paid off. He nonchalantly walked up to the painting and gave it just a cursory glance. He then, in an equally casual manner, walked into the office and booked a telephone line to bid for

Lot 124 for the following day's sale. Dealers will do this if they are unable to attend the sale in person, or wish to retain their anonymity. Anyway, at least it looked like I had got one dealer interested and it might sell; even if only at the lower end of the estimate. Others viewed the Stubbs, none of whom I recognised, but I was sure they could be agents representing either other major dealers or collectors. I was anticipating a bit of a surprise the following day.

Sale day arrived. We had a room full of people and by and large bidding was strong. Then it was time for the star lot; my mouth was dry and palms a little sweaty. Time to concentrate – there was business to be done.

'Lot 124, the sketch by Stubbs – where will you start me?'

Silence.

That didn't surprise me. I had a reserve of £50,000 and at this stage no interest at all – other than the man on the telephone. I started the bidding at £30,000 and looked in the saleroom for bidders.

Nothing.

Mild panic mixed with disappointment was beginning to take hold. Still, I had the gentleman on the telephone who I was sure would bid. I looked expectantly at my colleague taking the call and asked her if the dealer on the telephone wished to bid.

Nothing.

Why? Why would he book a phone line and not bid? My head was spinning. I had no option but to announce the painting as being unsold and move on to Lot 125. I was utterly confused and very upset. Where had it gone wrong? Had the Picture Man been mistaken? And, worst of all, what would Nimmy say? The remainder of the sale passed for me in a muddle of feelings ranging from exasperation to complete despondency.

The sale over, I couldn't put off telephoning Nimmy. After the general sale I had been only too keen to contact my client to give him the good news, but I was not looking forward to this conversation.

'Don't worry, dear boy; the good news is that Morris is now back running like a good 'un. I was really worried there for a time.'

'I'm really sorry, Nimmy, I just don't know where it all went wrong. What do you want me to do with it now?'

'Well, funnily enough I showed your catalogue to my young godson who is getting married and he was really quite taken with the old piccie. I think I might give it to him and his wife-to-be as a wedding present. In a way it would be lovely to keep it in the family as it were. Do let me know what I owe you for all your efforts; I'm very appreciative.'

What a gentleman.

Some two weeks later the Picture Man

came into the saleroom to look at four more little gems that I had been asked to sell.

'Rubbish, rubbish, not bad, rubbish.'

Normal service had been restored. I was still rather disappointed and embarrassed by my Stubbs failure so I asked him why he thought the trade had left it alone.

'You tried too hard to sell it. Should have just used your normal advert and not bothered to phone them up all the time. You put them off. They will buy because they want to, not because you want to sell it to them,' he replied in his usual pragmatic way.

So, that was a lesson learned. I wouldn't do that again. It was a good job I had had a client like Nimmy, otherwise I might well have been taken to task.

Lot 16

The Rat House

I hate rats. Nobody will ever convince me that they serve a useful purpose in life. Fortunately, since leaving my father's farm I had had little opportunity to test whether my phobia was as strong as ever. Until, that is, I was asked to clear a large town house in the middle of Worcester by the back of the railway station. My clients were acting as trustees for the elderly gentleman who lived there. The house, whose real name is irrelevant, was known in the city, and now always will be, as 'the Rat House'. The overgrown gardens were, so rumour had it, alive with the wretched rodents. Anyone asking directions was told to turn left past the Rat House, or go out of town past the Rat House. It had become part of the local folklore. As time passed various rumours were concocted as to what the inside might be like, for none of us, nor anyone we knew, had ever been inside. Little was I to know how aptly titled this crumbling old wreck was.

The house stood in a plot of nearly two acres in the centre of the city. As such its redevelopment value was enormous, but the old man who lived there would never entertain even the idea of selling it. He was almost totally reclusive, not speaking to any of his neighbours, barely ever venturing out. Some said that he had two children but they never seemed to visit the family home. The house had a number of outbuildings and stables but it was the gardens that first caught the eye. In fact the word garden conveyed quite the wrong impression: wilderness or jungle would have been a tad more accurate. Hacking a path through the brambles and overgrowth would have tested a group of SAS soldiers from the regiment in nearby Hereford. I had walked, and driven, past the property for years on my travels around the city and always wondered what the owner was like, what the contents were like and what sort of a story it told. Why had nothing ever been done to smarten it up or realise its potential?

I was delighted, therefore, to be given the opportunity to find the answers to some of these questions when a firm of solicitors asked me to act on behalf of the estate of the old man who had recently died. My professional delight was tinged with a touch of sadness, however, knowing that the old man had undoubtedly taken a number of secrets with him to the grave. The solicitors had given me a key to inspect the contents. They would then decide what course of action to take: either sell, or distribute to other members of the family if they existed. As I picked my way through the gardens, all sorts of notions flashed through my mind. Would I ever see my car and the office again? Perhaps creatures from the Middle Earth lived in the house. These fancies were exacerbated by a strange rustling sound which seemed to be coming from the debris that littered the garden. It was like a constant scratching noise echoing from the old pieces of corrugated sheets that lay around. It was all rather eerie. Rats; my skin started to itch and I was keen to reach the sanctuary of the house.

By the time I found the porch I was a bit jumpy. As I got to the front door further treats lay in store for me. Around the door was a sort of a wrought-iron veranda arrangement. It had a lead roof that in parts had vanished and in other parts had sagged and formed curious bowl-like shapes that collected rainwater rather than dispensing it through the gutter. This lead roof was supported by a metal structure, which in turn was raised on a wooden floor that all the gardening programmes on television refer to, rather smartly, as decking. Well, they hadn't seen this. It reminded me of that old schoolboy trick of putting a bucket of water on top of a slightly open door so that whoever walks through it knocks the water over and gets drenched. One foot on the so-called decking disturbed the metalware and moved the uprights, which in turn altered the pitch of the roof so that the water that had collected in the bowls overhead was instantly deposited on the person standing below. Obviously I only discovered this through first-hand experience. We had been through a severe drought – until the day before, when the heavens opened and un-loaded what seemed to be feet of rain. The bowls were full to overflowing. I must have put my foot on exactly the right – or wrong, depending on your viewpoint – board because the whole lot hit me like an icy blast from a fireman's hose. I wasn't so much wet as nearly drowned. My only consolation was that at least the water wasn't stagnant. I then put the key in the door and spent twenty minutes trying to open it until I discovered the key turned the lock only when it was put in upside down.

At last I got inside away from the dreaded rodents in the garden. The whole house was in semi-darkness as the shutters to all the windows were closed, and they looked to have been so for many years. I'm sure you will know that many of these old houses have huge, normally red velvet, curtains on metal poles fixed behind the front door. This was the next thing that hit me on the head: a rusty old pole followed by a mass of material that had accumulated what seemed to be a century's worth of dust and other unmentionables. After the water I felt as if I were being tarred and feathered. Either the house was keen to keep its secrets or it was waging a personal vendetta against me.

As I was picking myself up and dusting myself down in the hallway, I was sure I saw a brown cat run along the hall into the room at the far end. I supposed my next task was to find the wretched thing and let it out – I had no idea how long it had been locked in for. There was a strange, almost musty smell in the house and it felt as if I were walking on mulch that gardeners use on their flowerbeds. It was time to beat a retreat to the car for the torch that I should have brought with me in the first place.

I renegotiated the door, veranda and garden both ways without further mishap and, armed with my torch, found myself back in the hall.

I pushed the button on the torch and was mildly surprised that the batteries weren't flat, which was the usual problem with an article I used about twice a year. As my eyes gradually became accustomed to the fresh, bright light ... everything became horribly apparent.

The mulch underfoot looked very much like matt coloured chocolate peanuts. The last time I had seen these was when my father and I had lifted the floor of an old cattle pen on the farm to be confronted by a mass of rat droppings. There in front of me now was an even layer of such droppings. The musty smell obviously emanated from these and as for the brown cat... I stopped and tucked my trousers into my socks and took a deep breath that I instantly regretted. The smell was almost over-powering. I stood there wondering whether to go back to the office for the cavalry, but knew this would bring my manhood into question, so I decided to carry on.

The first door on the left was locked shut, the key still resting in the keyhole, and looked like it had been for some long time. As I moved down the passage-like hall, I found all the rooms off it were locked, except for the one at the end where my friend the 'cat' (well, it rhymes) had run. I decided to head for there. On the way I could see the hallway had holes in the floorboards that were the size of rabbit holes – I really didn't want to know what went on under these.

This end room was the kitchen. In it was a rear door to what was once a yard and presumably vegetable garden. After some fairly severe persuasion of the lock and bolt, the door opened, which had several effects. Fresh light came in to the room revealing its full glory, together with shafts of fresh air. Both of these were most welcome. The other effect that I secretly hoped for was that my little – or not so little – friend might be tempted to venture outside.

In some ways, however, illuminating the kitchen was a bad idea. Against one wall stood a wood-burning Aga-type stove. It was covered in grease and more of the 'mulch' and, judging by the scorch marks around it, it wasn't just wood-burning but also, wall-, ceiling- and floor-burning. The whole kitchen was fire-damaged and the musty smell was mingled, wholly unpleasantly, with that of smoke. As I looked around I saw several old painted pine cupboards and a set of stairs, which obviously wound their way up to the servants' quarters. I thought this was as good a place as any to start, so I climbed up the stairs, torch in hand. The small bedroom over the kitchen housed a Victorian brass four-poster bed with frayed drapes, which also smelled of smoke, and over where the head would have lain was the reason. The remains of a minor chimney fire where the chimney rose from the stove below were clearly visible.

I later discovered from the solicitor that the old man who had lived there only used the kitchen and the bedroom above, and the rest of the house was shut off. In his final days he had caused a chimney fire in the kitchen – of which I had seen the effects – and also received a nip on the face during the night from one of my rodent friends. I didn't find this out until after we had cleared the house, which was a good job or I would never have returned.

Moving back to the kitchen, I decided to open the cupboards and then wished I hadn't. The first was about six feet tall and three feet wide, with solid, painted blue doors. I opened them and worked my eyes down from the top shelf. The top was stacked with old pans, next were old biscuit tins – very old biscuit tins – and then below – horrors. The two bottom shelves were rats' nests. I was sure I saw one of the tins start to move. Was I imagining things? I slowly moved the tin forward and straight away regretted doing so. As I moved it I could see behind what looked like a long, thick strip of liquorice. The instant I realised it was a rat's tail coincided with the instant I leaped on to a fragile kitchen table and let out a rather girly scream that I'm pleased no one was there to hear. I later discovered the tins were gnawed and scratched on the outside by my furry friends trying to get at the food on the inside. This was turning out to be a daytime nightmare.

Having got this far I resolved to take the bull by the horns and explore the rest of the house. I walked back along the corridor and opened the door to what would have been the drawing room. Some of the keys resting in the locks at first proved difficult to turn but eventually they all became free. I would think I was the first human to venture inside for about twenty years. It was obvious the owners of the nests had been close to claiming squatters' rights throughout the house. It was evocative, somewhat, of Miss Havisham's house. Wallpaper was peeling off the walls, on which indiscernible paintings were hanging – in some cases literally, for the canvas had simply rotted out of the frames – and the furniture was covered in white, damp mildew spots. The furniture showed that the unmentionables weren't the only livestock in the house: it all looked like some particularly inaccurate darts players had used it for target practice. (This presence of woodworm was confirmed by little piles of timber dust under the furniture, which showed that it was very much active. People tend to get paranoid about the dreaded worm. My view is that you shouldn't overly worry about the holes – you only need get concerned when you see the dust or when the old worm has been so bad it has made the structure of the furniture fragile and unsafe.)

The sad thing was that the paintings, furniture and other objects in the house were good and the total neglect they had suffered had brought the values crashing down, sometimes to the point of worthlessness. It was the same story behind every door I opened. I found cobwebs so big that it looked as if the spiders had been working overtime for the last generation, with no time off for good behaviour. The bedrooms all contained lovely Victorian brass or mahogany beds and bedroom furniture – and all in the same appalling condition. I smiled briefly, thinking of polite society sleeping in these beds this time next year after I had sold them; if only they knew.

Everywhere I turned there were good pieces: Regency desks, First Period Worcester porcelain, and on the list went. This was going to take some sorting. The girls in the office, Sophie, Susie and Ella, weren't going to thank me for this, but we had to trawl through everything in the house. Experience had taught me that every drawer had to be opened and gone through. Finds for a country auctioneer rarely yield items worth lottery-winning sums, but things that fetch anything from tens of pounds to a few thousands. It all adds up, and you dare not miss anything. You never knew when you might find something that a collector would appreciate, which hadn't seen the light of day for a number of years. The excitement in this instance, however, was laced with a certain amount of trepidation as to what else we would discover.

Apparently all was not going to be that simple, for the old man did indeed have surviving relatives. His two children, a son and a daughter, who had had no contact with their father for the previous ten or twelve years, had now come out of the woodwork and war had broken out over what should happen to the estate. An estate that should prove to be sizeable, for not only was there the house and site with its development potential but also rumour abounded of valuable stocks and shares. I remembered an expression that I had first heard in the office of a Worcester lawyer: 'Where there's a will there's a relative.' Seemingly each sibling was claiming that the other had ignored their father and should therefore be struck out of the will, leaving everything to him, or her. To add to the lawyer's problem the will, which according to a file note had been made about ten years ago, had been made with his predecessor and now could not be found in the company's fireproof safe where, ironically, all wills were stored for safety reasons. This predecessor had died some five years ago and so there was no link at all with what had gone on before. It looked as if it would end up in court in an expensive legal battle that had every chance of costing the estate a fortune.

My concern while all this was going on was the security of the property – on two fronts. First, that more decay would occur to these potentially lovely contents, and second, that would-be burglars could view this as a wonderful opportunity and strip the house before we could do our job, a job that I was itching to carry out. I decided to let the lawyer know my views and telephoned him to arrange a meeting. During our telephone call I discovered that yet another spanner was being flung into the works. Our client's caring offspring were now considering taking legal action against his firm for losing the will. I couldn't help but feel sorry for the lawyer: we all get our share of awkward clients but every now and then, usually without warning, we walk into a minefield. I know I have on more than one occasion.

Our meeting had been fixed for some ten days later and I duly presented myself at the solicitors' offices. I was met by the lawyer looking as if he had just won the lottery. Apparently the offspring had each taken independent legal advice and agreed that the contents could be sorted and sold. Not only that, but to the lawyer's relief he had been given a further three months to try to find his client's elusive last will.

So now we could get on with our part in this little drama. We arrived at the house on the first morning ready to prepare receipts for the solicitors of all the items we would be taking. It was definitely a 'jeans and jumper job', and I had decided that cycle clips around the trouser legs was the better part of valour. I also had a large red spotted handkerchief around my mouth and nose which made me look like a cross between the Lone Ranger and a rather upmarket burglar. My mask had been liberally dosed in aftershave in an attempt to keep out the ghastly smell. Sophie, Susie and Ella thought I had gone a little over the top and were at great pains to tell me so. We decided to tackle one room at a time and remove all the more valuable items first. The drawing room was our first goal.

The door was slowly opened and the shutters, which had kept out the sunlight for many years, were eased fully open on their rusty, almost seized hinges. There was a huge fireplace with classical Minton tiles surrounding it, but what was more striking was the number of old birds' nests that had fallen down the chimney over the years. On the wall over the fire hung a wonderful Regency barometer. The brass circular dial was inscribed with the name of a London maker who worked in the city around 1815. Ordinarily a barometer like this would have sold for between £1,500 and £2,000. There was, however, a 'but' coming. The rosewood case, which had thick black veins in the deep brown timber, was riddled with woodworm. The pile of dust where the worm had been active resembled a termite hill. I gingerly picked up the barometer, only for the case nearly to crumble in my hands. The value now was probably below £100. From the ceiling a large nineteenth-century crystal glass chandelier was suspended; it was completely festooned with cobwebs which hung over it like a mosquito net in the jungle. A three-seater chesterfield in the middle of the room was upholstered in the brocade that the Victorians so loved. It was also absolutely filthy, and very much in our way.

It struck me all over again how extraordinary it was that the two children could ignore their father for such a long time and then expect to collect the jackpot now.

On the day in question Big Nige and Eric were on hand, ever happy to offer an opinion (as removal men often do). They were also helping to shift furniture so we could get around the house more easily. The chesterfield was hindering us and needed to be moved, so Nigel and Eric each grabbed an end and lifted it to take it into another room. They were shuffling the three yards towards the door into the hall, Eric walking backwards, when the unexpected happened. One of our rodent friends had decided to take a little nap in the upholstery at Nigel's end of the chesterfield. The movement had obviously woken it from its slumbers and it fell out on to the floor, shook itself and ran towards Eric. Now Eric was not known for his speed but I have never seen anyone move so quickly. This rat was enormous. The first I had seen at the house was big enough but this one was the size of fat brown Yorkshire terrier. As the rat ran through Eric's legs, he dropped his end of the chesterfield and sprinted up the sofa, which was at an angle of 45 degrees, as Nigel had been unaware of what had happened and was still holding his end upright. He was suddenly confronted by Eric, about six inches from his nose, in a pair of bright red glasses. Sophie, Susie and Ella were in tears of laughter while I had leaped on to a chair. After that incident I decided to give Big Nige and Eric a little more space in case anything else unexpected might happen, though I have to say that Eric seemed to develop a most peculiar gait – almost that of a man with very bandy legs walking on eggshells.

The reason for moving the sofa was to look at a good Regency rosewood card table decorated with an ornate brass inlay. From a distance it looked to have escaped the ravages of woodworm. It had – but not the damp atmosphere. When I placed a hand on the veneer it fell off in huge lumps and I immediately saw the legs were starting to rot. This would require complete, sensitive and expensive restoration before it could be offered on the retail market.

This was the story throughout the Rat House: crumbling treasures that were starting a new life for the first time in possibly fifty years. It took some weeks to go through, catalogue and remove to storage the myriad articles in the house. The card table was the most expensive item but there were numerous boxes of goodies in the sales that sold for between £5 and £100. The dealers and collectors alike who attended our sales always searched eagerly through these boxes, looking for those fresh-to-the-market goods that were so sought after and choice little gems that would add to any collection. The contents of the house eventually sold for a figure in excess of £30,000 – a huge sum of money – but I have always wondered what they would have made if they had been in even slightly better condition.

The real end to the story came when I saw the lawyer acting for the estate of the old man one lunchtime in Worcester. He had found the will at last and the two children did indeed get a mention. They were left £5,000 each, with the balance of the estate being left to local charities. When the property had been sold, together with various shares and other assets, this realised over £2½ million.

Lot 17

Big Nige's Chest

This was beginning to get quite worrying: we had not seen any sign of human life for about half an hour and even the sheep were now few and far between. The mobile phone was completely useless: the final semblance of any signal had disappeared about the time we had passed the last house.

'We' were Sophie, myself and Big Nige and we were somewhere in the middle of the

Brecon Beacons on our way to meet a new client; that's if we could ever find her. We were in the accepted (or should that be dreaded) mode of transport of anyone with even the remotest interest in the antiques business – a Volvo estate. Our journey had originated in a telephone call from a local accountant in Worcester who wanted me to contact his maiden great-aunt who, ten years ago at the age of seventy-three, had decided to drop out to pursue her interest in painting. Her family had now decided that she lived in too remote a location to be on her own at eighty-three and, against her will, felt it was time for her to move closer to her family. From her great-nephew's description, Hester Jevereaux sounded a very independent lady. Aunt Hettie, as she was apparently known to one and all, did nothing to dispel this image when I telephoned to make an appointment to go to see her.

'The family thinks I need to move – stuff and nonsense if you ask me. You'd better come and see me; I'm free next Tuesday after lunch. I'll write to you with directions.'

The letter duly arrived. The postmark had some unbelievably long Welsh place name that was totally unpronounceable and the handwriting was equally tricky. In fact the letter could well have been written in ancient Greek for all the sense it made. It didn't look too dissimilar to the printout from a hospital heart monitor. I thought I had better telephone her again just to make sure I had got everything right.

'Did you not get my letter? I thought I had made it quite clear.'

'Er, yes... but I foolishly spilled my coffee all over it and it was a little tricky to read.'

I thought that was an inspired but still tactful response. I fear Aunt Hettie saw through me at once.

'Humph' – at least that's what it sounded like – followed by, 'Well, it's quite simple.'

Words that, as usual, struck terror into my heart. I scribbled down in careful detail the route we were to take.

Aunt Hettie also told me that she had a small antique chest that she wanted to sell straight away, which should fit in the back of my car. And she wanted me to recommend a haulier who could not only transport to the saleroom the items that she wanted to sell but also move her to 'wherever my wretched family think I should now live'. That explained Big Nige's presence. Sophie was there for moral support: being a coward when dealing with a lady who had already intimidated me, I felt the female touch might be a help.

Timekeeping is not one of my strongest points but this was one appointment I did not want to be late for. Aunt Hettie had said the journey from Worcester should take about two hours. I thought it best to allow two and a half and told Big Nige not to be late. He did not let me down and for once it looked like I might be on time.

We arrived on the outskirts of Brecon pretty much on schedule; now it was time to study Aunt Hettie's directions. I have said before that grass growing in the middle of the road is a sure sign that the earth is flat and the road is just about to fall off the edge. This was one of those roads. On it went and up we climbed. And up. And up. The road – or track would have been a better term – got steeper and steeper and it would have been well suited to test-driving Land-Rovers. As we drove, Big Nige sat in the back of the car whistling away, without a care in the world. His sense of melody was the wrong side of tone deaf, but unfortunately he thought he was mighty tuneful. His favourite songs were the Beatles' but I'm not sure how Lennon and McCartney would have viewed his interpretations of their greatest hits. He somehow managed to mix all their songs together at once, with sorry results.

The road wound up and up and reached the point where the view over the bonnet ceased to be the grey of the tarmacked road ahead; now all that was in sight was the clear blue sky over the radiator. Not reassuring. The car seemed to be at a similar angle to the space shuttle on the launch pad. I didn't see how we could continue such an ascent for much longer without Sherpa Tensing dishing out the oxygen masks. We had long since left behind any sign of human habitation; if the SAS trained in this part of the world I could fully understand why they are the feared force that they are.

At long last the road levelled out and we found ourselves on top of the Beacons themselves. The view ahead was crystal clear: all greens and blues and nothing else. No buildings, no people, no animals, no nothing – just sky and grass. On we drove. I was praying that the car didn't break down otherwise I could see us being stranded here without food and with no hope of escape. The Serrell imagination was again working overtime. The other two occupants of the car seemed unconcerned by our impending doom. Sophie said she was really enjoying the view and that this was God's own country while Big Nige whistled – or murdered – his private 'Yellow Submarine'/'Yesterday' arrangement. The pair of them had simply no imagination or concept of the perils that could befall us. The track ahead seemed to meander on and on; there weren't even any turn-offs or junctions to offer an alternative. We had no option but to continue. It was not just a question of finding Aunt Hettie's; any house at all would have been a bonus. At long last we arrived at a crossroads; sadly the directions I had taken down during our telephone call had long since been discarded. I stopped and thought for a moment; straight on seemed to me to be the logical option. However the other two finally decided to voice their opinions.

'I should hang a left,' came from Big Nige at the same time as Sophie offered, 'It's bound to be right.' I exercised the boss's prerogative and drove straight on.

After what seemed like miles we saw farm buildings in the distance.

'Doesn't look much like an artist's retreat to me – more like a smelly old farm,' coupled with, 'I'm in the haulage business; I've got a nose for directions – we should have gone left.' My two passengers were being helpful again.

We pulled into the yard and stopped; we had no option as the track was a dead-end. The place was like the *Marie Celeste*: completely deserted. I thought it prudent to stay in the car and suggested to Big Nige that he should go and see if he could find a friendly native.

'Nope, not a soul.' He gave me a mutinous stare. 'We should have gone left.'

I resisted getting tetchy, turned the car around and headed back to the crossroads. I didn't wait for Big Nige to voice his opinion again but indicated towards his choice well before the junction. We had only gone about half a mile when the road dipped into a slight hollow that was invisible from the crossroads and, lo and behold, there was our destination.

'You should always listen to a removal man – it's like an inbuilt sixth sense.'

Possibly, but crowing is never attractive.

We pulled up and got out of the car. The house was an attractive stone cottage with 360-degree views over the surrounding countryside. I recall reading somewhere that the distance to the horizon is about eight miles; well, here it seemed to exceed that by far. There was a valley below in which for the first time in what seemed like hours we could see other traffic. Suddenly there was the roar of a jet; bizarrely it flew along underneath us. We made our way to the front door. I was just about to knock when the door opened, revealing a Margaret Rutherford lookalike doing her best Miss Marple impression; Aunt Hettie certainly had presence.

'Given you up for lost,' she barked.

'I'm awfully sorry; I think I must have totally misread your directions.'

This time her reply was clearly a derisive, 'Humph.'

There wasn't much I could say to that; without words she seemed to have said everything.

Aunt Hettie wore a thick Guernsey sweater, corduroy trousers, heavy brogues and a fiercely intelligent expression. No crimes would have gone unsolved in her neighbourhood – that is if there had been anyone around to commit them. Her cottage was in a truly magnificent setting. Today it was glorious with the sun shining and the birds singing. However when the wind blew and the rain and snow fell perhaps it would not have been quite so idyllic. There were no buildings, hills or other land-forms to pro-tect it from the weather. My family always referred to the type of wind that would blow here as a lazy one: it would rather go through you than take the trouble to go round you. To the side of the cottage was Aunt Hetty's transport: a series one Land-Rover, built in about 1949. It was in pristine condition but did not offer much in the way of creature comforts. I remarked that I thought it was lovely.

'Bought her new after the war; just cost me more to restore her than I paid for her. But she's never let me down, which is more than can be said for most things in life.'

This Parthian shot left me feeling a little intimidated; I don't know why, she was a lovely lady, it was just that I hoped that I wasn't going to let her down. Eventually we made our way into the cottage where Big Nige and Sophie (naturally) soon had her eating out of their hands.

'Do come in, dears; would you like tea?' And almost as an afterthought, 'You as well, Mr Serrell?' I generally don't like being called Mr Serrell; only bank managers and tax inspectors address me thus. This only made me feel more nervous.

Once inside the cottage it was obvious that she was a keen artist; examples of her work hung throughout her home. Very keen indeed, but her enthusiasm was inversely proportional to her skill. To be blunt, she had none whatsoever. Most of her work was of the local landscape but could easily have been an abstract subject. Rather than a hair brush and a palette knife it looked as if she used a four-inch plaster brush and a spade. Inevitably she asked the question that we all dread when talking to an enthusiastic amateur.

'What do you think of my work; what would it sell for in the saleroom?'

There was a pause while I tried to think of a response that was plausible but hid my true thoughts. Before I had composed one she said, 'About fourpence I would have thought – they're awful. But it does give me real pleasure to paint.'

'Well, that's the main thing,' I replied, relieved that I didn't have to give my view, and embarrassed for her as her work really was not good.

She went on, 'You'll be delighted to know you haven't got to sell any of my masterpieces. I should like to show you around so you can see what the job entails. Also we can look at the small chest in the hall which I want you to take back with you.' We walked into the hall.

Bloody hell, was my reaction on two counts. First, it was a good piece of furniture and, second, small it was not. My place in the car was booked as I was the driver and so was the chest's, for it was far too good to consider leaving behind. That left one seat for Sophie and Big Nige. I thought I would leave it to them to fight it out. One of them would have to stop with Aunt Hettie.

She looked at Big Nige, obviously deciding to cut me, the middle man, out, and said, 'Will you get it in the car all right?'

'Can do,' replied the jolly giant. He had clearly lost control of all his faculties. Maybe it was the lack of oxygen.

'Excellent, let me go and make the tea,' our host said as she wandered into the kitchen, leaving the three of us staring at the 'small chest'. It was a Dutch dressing table fitted with three drawers and had a mirror superstructure on top. The timber, which was mahogany, was covered with a decorative inlay of veneers of different coloured timbers, showing birds, leaves and flowers. Such

251

decoration is known as marquetry. Parquetry is a similar form of inlay but is of geometric design; hence the term parquet in parquet flooring. The reason I was so keen to take it back with us that night – sacrificing one of my two travelling companions if necessary – was that I felt it would make between £3,000 and £5,000 in the saleroom.

Out of earshot of Aunt Hettie I said to Big Nige, 'How the hell are we going to get it and, more importantly from your point of view, you two in the car?'

'You worry too much. We'll get her in.' I wasn't sure whether Big Nige's last remark was addressed to the chest or Sophie. He went on, 'May as well make a move with her now.' I still wasn't sure who the 'her' was but he grabbed one end of the chest and indicated to Sophie and me that we should lift up the other end.

We carried the chest outside and put it down by the back of the Volvo. It seemed to get bigger rather than smaller during its short journey outside and I didn't share Big Nige's conviction that it would go in easily; certainly not without the aid of a chainsaw.

'Phil, you're gonna have to drop the back seat.' So where were the two of them going to sit? I thought. I never had Big Nige down as a mind-reader but, as if by magic, he continued, 'Soph can sit in the front and I'll balance in the back with the chest.'

We did manage to get the chest into the back of the car; in fact it wasn't a problem (I had been fretting unnecessarily – again). Where Big Nige was going to go, however, was something of a mystery. The only free space was a strip about twelve inches wide running along the side of the car. Being six feet four inches tall and the thick end of eighteen stone it was going to be tight if not impossible. Still, at least we had got the chest in.

We made our way back into the cottage and inspected the other items that Aunt Hettie wanted to sell. Strangely, though not uniquely, the chest was the only stick in the house that was worth anything at all. Like many arty people, her furniture was purely functional and lacked any real value. Big Nige made his arrangements with our client to move her lock, stock and barrel to her new home with the surplus bits coming to the saleroom. I was at some pains to point out that while the chest in the car was good the remaining contents of the house probably wouldn't get anywhere near it in terms of value. Indeed, it would cost more to move than it would make. Aunt Hettie, ever the realist, was fully aware of that.

'Was left the chest by my godfather, the rest of my furniture does its job, which is all I need. It doesn't have to be valuable.'

When it was time to leave I was hoping

that we could make our own way out to the car. I was still concerned as to how we were going to fold Big Nige into the back and was not overly keen for Aunt Hettie to witness the performance. But no such luck. There was a decided twinkle in her eye when she announced, 'I am going to have to come out and see how you're all going to fit into the car with the chest already in there.'

So there was no way I could hide our struggles. We stood outside the car. Sophie being Sophie, she leaped into the front passenger seat and pretended that nothing was amiss. I opened the back of the car and looked at Big Nige. He reminded me of a Great Dane attempting to get into a Jack Russell terrier's bed, trying to make himself look as small as possible in the process. He was not cut out to be a circus contortionist but somehow managed to thread himself along the side of the chest in the car. As soon as he was even remotely settled I slammed the rear door down, only just missing his feet. I bid Aunt Hettie farewell and quickly drove off. After we had gone about a mile up the road a pitiful cry came from the back of the car, 'Bloody hell, you'd better stop and back up a bit.'

'Why's that, Nige?' I said, puzzled.

''Cos I think you missed a pothole just then and you've managed to find every other one since we left: I don't want it to feel left out.' This rare turn of sarcastic wit from the big boy was quickly followed by a more straightforward, 'Oww, bloody hell.'

'What's the matter now, Nige?'

'You found the last bump and now I've got one of the drawer knobs stuck in the small of me back.'

I did feel sorry for poor Nige. I glanced in the rear-view mirror and could see him completely wedged into the side of the car. He looked like a hippopotamus stuck in a rabbit hole. Still, on the plus side, at least it had stopped him whistling. The journey home was relatively uneventful for Sophie and me in the front of the car but our conversation was regularly interrupted by cries of pain from the back as various parts of the chest embedded themselves into Nige's anatomy. On arrival at the sale-room Sophie and I quickly lifted the back of the car and pulled the chest out. Big Nige was barely able to move let alone get out; he was welded to the side with the rear window winder sticking into his nose.

It was all worth while, though, as it was a cracking piece of furniture, and once photographed and adorning the cover of the next sale catalogue it looked better than ever. It was no surprise that it created a lot of interest from dealers at the sale preview and was keenly bid on by a number of them. Big Nige, rarely for him, came to the sale to see how the pain-in-the-neck chest (as he now referred to it) sold. The hammer eventually fell at £4,300 and I was pleased with the result.

My concern now was what on earth I would do with the rest of Aunt Hettie's stuff once Nigel had moved her to her new home and we had the surplus in the saleroom. But in the end there was no problem – and no surplus. As Aunt Hettie succinctly put it: 'My mothering family can whistle, I'm not moving and that's the end of that.'

Lot 18

'Don't Worry, It's Only Mother Breathing'

Valuations can serve many different purposes. A probate valuation is required by the executors of a deceased's estate; this is because tax is payable on the value of an estate and has to be calculated on the total value of all items forming part of the estate in question. A family division valuation may be required to share out property amicably or, more unpleasantly, for an acrimonious divorce settlement. Valuation for insurance is yet another form. For this purpose the cost of replacing antiques lost or damaged by fire, burglary or other causes is calculated. An insurance company will then reach a settlement with the insured based on the valuation. Many clients do not realise that in these circumstances it is the responsibility of the insured to prove the value of the loss.

Most auctioneers, and some dealers, will carry out all these kinds of valuations, which are normally in writing, for a fee. The fee is based on a percentage of the valuation total; it does not take a genius to work out that the higher the valuation, the higher the fee. All reputable auctioneers and dealers ignore this element when preparing their report but I have occasionally seen valuations where the figures have seemed surprisingly high; no doubt with the accompanying fee note in mind.

In this business jobs are a little like buses: nothing comes along for ages and then you are overrun by the wretched things. About five years ago I was instructed to deal with an example of each type of valuation within the space of a week. And each of them was, shall we say, a little out of the ordinary.

Evie Jenkins was a lovely old lady who, at the ripe old age of eighty-three, had moved upstairs, as it were. Her two daughters were now in the process of winding up her estate and I had been instructed by them to act in respect of her personal chattels. Gavina and

Robina were in their early fifties and late forties respectively and clearly from the same stable. They each had a trim figure and dressed in a timeless and sophisticated way, and, while they could not be described as beauties, there was something about them that separated them from the crowd. They were both striking to look at, with strong cheekbones and piercing blue eyes. In character, however, they were as different as chalk and cheese. Gavina worked with the local travelling library, ran the Sunday school and was a regular at church. Robina was something of an enigma; no one was sure exactly what she did but, judging by the exotic holidays she took three or four times a year, she was clearly making a success of it. There was even a suggestion that she had a number of wealthy boyfriends that the less charitable referred to as clients.

I met them at their late mother's home, a small bungalow in Worcester. It was similar to the properties either side of and opposite it; it did not stand out in any way at all in its tranquil street. But as soon as I was guided into the sitting room I sensed what my grandmother used to call an atmosphere. Gavina seemed a bag of nerves. In contrast Robina was determinedly cool and could have charmed the birds off the wallpaper that decorated the walls.

For probate valuations all the assets of the

deceased have to be taken into account. That means absolutely everything. Quality and quantity are irrelevant: it is the global total that is paramount. When I prepare reports of this type I always ask for all the goods and chattels that formed part of the estate to be pointed out to me. The little bungalow was clean and tidy but undoubtedly a little tired – it had not been decorated for some time. There were tell-tale marks on the walls where pictures had recently been removed, and behind the mantelpiece the outline of a clock that had obviously sat there for some time but was now nowhere to be seen. Wherever you looked there were similar outlines that really did give the game away. Some of Evie's personal chattels had been removed in the very recent past. I asked the obvious question as tactfully as I could.

'I presume that you've taken some bits away for safekeeping?'

'Yes, sort of,' said Gavina.

Simultaneously Robina said, 'No, nothing at all.'

This was not going to be easy. I could only value what I could see and my role was not that of a tax inspector, but it was painfully evident that items had been spirited away.

'Look, there's clearly a bit of confusion here. I need to pop out to the car to get my books and notepad. You have a chat and let me know what you want me to look at when

I get back.'

I went out to my car wondering whether Gavina's conscience would get the better of Robina's creative instincts. I thought it politic to leave it a few minutes before returning. After a suitable period of time had elapsed I returned, fascinated to discover the outcome of the family debate.

'Robby's taken a few bits of Mummy's for safe-keeping but we can arrange to bring them to your saleroom one day for you to have a look at.'

One–nil to Gavina, a result I would not have predicted. I could see Robina's composed façade had slipped. She now looked more like a naughty schoolgirl who has just been discovered stealing sweets from the tuck shop. The further I penetrated into the house the clearer it became how ruthless she had been. There were outlines on walls throughout the property where Robina had, so she thought, subtly removed her mother's possessions so that they could not be included in the valuation. Behind the door in the dining room was even the shadow of a longcase clock that was no longer present. I made a schedule of the items that remained and arranged to meet the two ladies at the saleroom to value the items that Robina had removed for 'safe-keeping'.

A week later, at the duly appointed time, a transit van, hired from the local car and van rental company, arrived at the saleroom. I was unsure what was being delivered, certainly no deliveries were expected, just Gavina and Robina with the 'few' possessions they had removed from their mother's. I was a little taken aback when the two ladies got out of the van. Surely they couldn't have taken so much away that it needed a van to deliver it all? Robina was looking quite contrite, saying little, and walking in a way that only she could, with her hands clasped dramatically behind her head.

'Good morning, ladies. I'll put the coffee on and get someone to help you bring the bits in.' The atmosphere once again seemed rather chilly as the two sisters walked into the saleroom and I thought if I left them alone for a little it might improve matters. I made myself scarce for fifteen minutes and caught up on some messages in the office. When I felt enough time had passed I made my way back into the saleroom to the tables that we had laid out ready to display Evie's belongings.

As I cast my eye over the items in front of me I realised that Robina had a very good eye; she had, by accident or design, been extremely professional in her selection. There were three paintings worth about £2,000 each by Oliver Clare, a Birmingham artist who was well known for his still-life studies of fruit, and equally well known for enjoying a drink and swapping his work for alcohol. Two small vases from the local Royal Worcester porcelain factory painted with pheasants by James Stinton would also have made the thick end of £1,000 each. The clock that must have sat on the mantelpiece was not startling: a glitzy thing imitating a Sèvres ormolu clock with blue decorated porcelain panels in a gilt metal case. My father would have referred to it as 'all fur coat and no knickers'. The longcase clock from behind the door had an oak case with a painted enamel dial and a thirty-hour movement. Clocks of this type normally have thirty-hour or eight-day movements; this simply indicates how often they need to be wound. These two were worth about £300 and £600 respectively.

I trawled my way through everything and estimated that the value of the goods removed for safe-keeping was just over £15,000. The attitude of the two sisters was once again in sharp contrast: Gavina seemed relieved that all was out in the open, while Robina appeared totally uninterested. Throughout the whole performance she had hardly said a word. Oddly enough she continued to hold her arms in the baggy jumper she was wearing high in the air with her hands firmly clasped together behind her head. She remained aloof from the whole proceedings.

'Is that it then – finished?' she said disdainfully.

Sulking like a scolded child, I thought; the sooner this job was over and out of the way the better.

'I think so, Philip; thank you so much for your help and for being so understanding.' Gavina was a charming lady and clearly embarrassed by her sister's behaviour. 'Wait a minute. Robina, where are those sweet little silver sauce boats?'

'Which sauce boats?' Robina replied. She had undoubtedly stiffened. Immediately the atmosphere turned several degrees cooler – positively frosty.

'You know, the ones you said you always wanted. Where are they?'

No response. Robina stared towards the saleroom ceiling, elbows still at the same level as her shoulders. She looked like a 1950s Hollywood film starlet in a moody pose. I looked from one sister to the other, utterly at a loss. Eventually Gavina broke the awkward silence.

'Robina, why are you holding your arms up high like that?'

This was a question I had been longing to ask but hadn't been able to work it into the conversation. It was hardly relevant to the job in hand.

'I don't know what you're talking about.'

It did seem awfully strange that Robina

had held this pose for the whole time she had been with me in the saleroom. Suddenly Gavina realised why.

'Robina, you've got something hidden in that jumper. It's the sauce boats, isn't it?'

Of course. I held my breath. What would – or could – Robina do now? Shrugging, her face still full of disdain, she lowered her arms. A Georgian silver sauce boat slowly slid down each of the baggy sleeves and into her hands.

She didn't seem at all embarrassed but strangely I was. I gently took them from her, put a price on them and escaped, hastily making my apologies for leaving the two of them to pack everything up again and remove it from the saleroom.

I was glad that job was over; I hate being the middle man while families argue over their dead relatives' possessions. It never ceases to amaze me the lengths some people will go to, to get what they want.

The next day I was due at a house in Shropshire to value its contents on a family division basis. I had been instructed by a firm of solicitors from Shrewsbury to provide a valuation for the two sisters who owned the contents between them; one sister lived at the house with her husband and she wished to buy out her sister's half share at a fair price. This couldn't be too problematical: a simple valuation and only two parties involved. My letter of instruction advised that I was to meet a Mr Smit, the husband of the sister in residence. I smiled as I reflected on the lawyer's letter; it wasn't only me who got things wrong. His secretary had missed the 'h' off Smith; such signs of human failing always made me feel better as I constantly seemed to make similar mistakes. I reasoned that as the solicitors were based in Shrewsbury they had come to me as I was 'off the patch' and would therefore be seen as totally impartial, not knowing either of the parties. I pulled up at the house looking forward to a quiet and stress-free job after the rigours of dealing with Robina and Gavina. I turned the engine off and slowly got out of the car.

'You bloody clear off.'

The voice came from a first-floor window.

'I'm Philip Serrell, I'm here to do a valuation. Is Mr Smith in?'

'No need no bloody valuation. I Smit. You bloody clear off.'

Here we go again, I thought. Whatever happened to the simple life?

'Look, Mr Smith, why don't you telephone the lawyers. They'll tell you why I'm here.'

'I SMIT and no bloody need telephone lawyers. You bloody clear off – now.'

I was about to try to reason with him when he ranted on, 'You bloody clear off now or I bloody shoot you.' And at that he produced a shotgun. Being shot at was not in my job description and was certainly something I had had no training for.

Discretion took the better part of valour and I retreated smartly to the driver's seat of my car. I sat there for a few moments wondering what to do next when my mind was made up for me.

'I bloody shoot if you don't bloody clear off now.'

Hardly a reasoned argument but a particularly persuasive one. I started the engine and drove off wondering what on earth I had got myself into now.

Shrewsbury was about five miles away and I decided I would drive to the lawyers' offices and find out what was going on. I found them quite easily, parked the car and made my way to their reception. I explained my predicament and asked to see the person dealing with my new-found friend. I must have looked as shaken as I felt, for I was brought a cup of the very sweet tea normally reserved for victims of severe shock. I don't actually like sweet tea but drank it gratefully none the less. A distinguished grey-haired gentleman in an immaculate pinstripe suit with highly polished black shoes appeared.

'I'm so sorry, Mr Serrell, I'm really terribly sorry. Please come into my office.'

I followed him into a dark, oak-panelled

office that was furnished with lovely old nineteenth-century desks and chairs.

'Do sit down and let me explain.' I sat in a beautiful Georgian mahogany-framed armchair that I couldn't help thinking would do well in my next sale. 'Franz Smit is the husband of one of the two sisters in this matter. He is Austrian and came over here during the war. The two sisters get on famously and have decided that it's time to finalise the distribution of the contents of the old family home. That's why we need your valuation. But Mrs Smit can't seem to get through to her husband that even though the contents of the house need to be valued there is no way that they will be removed or sold. He seems to think it's the first step to him losing his home. Nonsense, of course, but there we are.'

I explained that in Worcestershire we were a little old-fashioned and that being shot at was not generally seen as being part of the job.

'I'm really sorry about that. I toyed with the idea of warning you that Mr Smit might be a little difficult but I genuinely thought it would all blow over. I should have guessed really when none of the local firms would take on the job.'

So much for coming to me for 'off the patch impartiality'. The local boys had local knowledge and just didn't fancy being used

267

as target practice. A view I shared.

'Look, if you can give me about half an hour I'll speak to Mrs Smit – she works in the town – and see if she can placate her husband enough for you to do the job this afternoon. Obviously we'll pay your fee accordingly.'

Well, there didn't seem much more I could do, so I arranged to reappear in about an hour's time. On my return Mrs Smit was waiting with the lawyer.

'Mr Serrell, I'm so, so sorry. My husband is convinced that everything is to be taken away from us. He doesn't seem to understand that half of the furniture in the house is my sister's. My sister married well and while I was left the house in my late father's will the contents were left to us jointly. My sister is very relaxed about the whole position and it's really my wish that we should sort things out now. Perhaps if I came with you it might ease the situation a little.'

I was all for the situation being eased and agreed to her suggestion.

As I drove her back to the house Mrs Smit apologised every other mile for her husband's behaviour. She was so clearly devastated that I found myself saying, 'It's all part of the job.' I could hardly believe my ears.

On seeing his wife Mr Smit's whole demeanour changed. He was a lion that

268

roared when she was not around but turned into a mouse in her presence.

Once inside the house I couldn't believe my eyes. Mr Smit had been so protective I was expecting to see rooms full of precious antiques and fine art. In fact there was nothing there of an antique nature at all. Nothing I would have wanted as a gift and definitely nothing that warranted getting shot for. My valuation of the contents of the whole house came out a little shy of £4,000. One and a half per cent of £4,000 worked out at £60. Love of the job was apparently not the only thing I had inherited from Ernest Edward Foley Rayer: I didn't seem to be able to charge proper fees either. Ah well, on to the next.

This was an insurance valuation on the outskirts of Bromsgrove, some ten miles more or less due north of the county town. I had arranged to meet the son of the lady whose house I was to visit to prepare the valuation. The son, a Mr Andrew Player, was about forty-five, the same age as me, and had been quite precise on the telephone in what he wanted me to do. Apparently his mother had never had the contents of her home insured properly, let alone valued, and he felt it was high time this was remedied. I could do nothing but applaud this sentiment. When I pulled into the parking area of a 1930s detached house on an estate of similar, and, dare I say, architecturally uninspiring houses, nothing seemed out of the ordinary.

'Good morning, Mr Serrell. Good of you to come.' His voice was very quiet, not at all how I remembered it on the telephone, almost a whisper. I imagined he had been stricken with some form of laryngitis that was doing the rounds.

'Mother is upstairs in bed.' I struggled to hear what he said; observing this, he repeated himself. Well, that wasn't too irregular; she would surely have been seventy-odd years old and if she wanted a lie-in that was fine by me.

'Perhaps we had better start there.' I thought this was a little odd, and didn't want Mrs Player to rush out of her bed on my account.

'No, don't worry, we can start down here and work our way upstairs when she gets up.' It really made little difference to me where we started and I wasn't about to put his mother out when there was clearly no need.

'Mr Serrell, you don't understand, my mother is dying.'

Well, that made me feel more than a little uncomfortable. What would he think of me calling at a time like this? She must have been unwell when the appointment had been made and worsened considerably since. Poor Mr Player must have forgotten all about me calling – yet strangely he hadn't seemed too surprised when he first let me into the house. I was rather confused. His remark proved something of a conversation stopper. I never know what to say in circumstances like these. I always felt my professional training should have included a short course in bedside manners; auctioneers, in the process of clearing deceaseds' estates, often find themselves in situations where tact and kid gloves are required. This was clearly one of them.

'I'm terribly sorry. Would it be more convenient if I came back another day?' I asked, trying to be thoughtful. This must be a distressing time for Mr Player.

'No, I'm sorry, you don't understand, my mother is dying now. We'll do her room first, just in case. Better to do it now; it might be a bit tricky if anything does happen. She's not expected to last the day.'

Well, the young Mr Player might not have been feeling put out or awkward but I certainly did. If I felt uncomfortable before, now I felt absolutely terrible. I once had to do a valuation of an undertaker's premises and the presence of the recently departed did nothing to sharpen my skills as a valuer. Yet despite some nifty footwork – I've always prided myself on being a quick thinker – no matter what I suggested Mr Player was adamant that the job should go ahead.

'It would be what Mother wanted,' he

insisted. In her present state I could think of numerous other things that would have been top of my wish list. But with that he set off up the stairs and I was left to follow. He strode into the bedroom at the top of the stairs; I waited outside just in case the worst had happened – something that did not appear to have occurred to my client.

'Come on in, Mr Serrell. I think there's a chest of drawers that you might find quite interesting.'

Under normal circumstances he would have been right: it was an early Georgian walnut chest. It looked as if it had been got at about eighty years ago by an enthusiastic restorer but fretting about that was not top of my list of priorities at that particular moment.

On the pillow I could see the head of a frail old lady with a shock of white hair. She lay motionless and I keenly watched the bedclothes to see if they were moving up and down. Was she still breathing? Nothing. I really didn't want to be here.

'Look, Mr Player, do you not think it would be better if I came back another day?'

'No, it'll be fine. I've had a day off work and I can't really afford to waste the time.'

He was proving to be a really caring son. At that the head on the bed made a noise like a loosely stringed banjo being plucked. I must have jumped about two feet up in the air before I was reassured by the son: 'Don't worry, it's only Mother breathing.'

Aghast, I stared at Mr Player as he carried on: 'My grandfather bought it for my parents as a wedding present and it has always been something I have admired.'

I was so concerned with Mrs Player that I hadn't got a clue what he was talking about. 'Pardon?'

'The chest, Mr Serrell, it's lovely, isn't it? Do you think the handles are original?'

I neither knew nor cared. I just wanted to get out of the house as quickly as possible. I went through the valuation almost in a trance and truthfully can remember very little of what I saw. Normally I'm hopeless at recalling people but am pretty good with their possessions. In this case the reverse was true. I left the house with Mr Player still muttering in my ear about the originality of the handles on the bedroom chest.

The telephone rang a week later in the office.

'Mr Serrell, Player here. Mother has died but I wondered if you could possibly make your fee note out to her estate. It might just help a little – I can set it off against dues payable.'

I was staggered: people never ceased to amaze me.

In one week I reckon I had experienced a broad range of human emotions and witnessed an equally broad range of behaviour. It was time to get back to the relative normality of the saleroom.

Lot 19

A Tale of Two Tables

This was just about the worst part of the job. I hated telling clients that their pride and joy, on which I was being asked to pass an opinion, was worth little or nothing. I had a colleague, some years ago, who was known in the office as 'Good News Geoff': if there was any bad news coming, he was not the man to deliver it. Geoff was a good friend, and if someone was in line for promotion or due a pay rise he was always keen to break the news personally. When, however, the scenario was not quite so rosy, and redundancy or a severe pay cut was in order, Geoff always seemed to have an important client to see and I got to deliver the bad news. But this time there was no one else who might even possibly shoulder the burden for me.

As a country auctioneer, it gave me a buzz to discover something interesting and valuable, but that didn't always happen. And if people really needed good news I reckoned it was my job to take the blow with them when it wasn't forthcoming. Walter, standing patiently opposite me, was waiting for me to tell him that his dining-room table – a family heirloom – was worth a fortune. And how he needed it to be.

Walter was a lovely man. He lived with his wife and three sons in the wilder part of Herefordshire, where they all eked out something just short of a living. Walter's father and grandfather had been clients of my first boss, Mr Rayer. He tended to have a huge influence on the people whose lives he touched, and he invariably elicited loyalty and respect from those who knew him. Such loyalty was a trait prominent in Walter and his forefathers. The farming fraternity has always been resistant to change, and never more so than in respect to their professional advisers. Walter, true to type, had remained faithful to the firm that had advised his family through the generations. Over the years most of the good things in the family home had been sold to supplement the meagre income that the farm provided, and now here we were, all standing around this table, staring at Walter's last hope.

The voice that came out of his huge frame was almost a whisper. It was as faded as the frayed check shirt he wore tucked into equally well-loved corduroy trousers that had more patches than original material.

Walter's wife had standards and her laundry was first class, for his clothes smelled strongly of fresh soap. But it was his tie that set off the whole ensemble. I knew of few farmers who wore a tie, other than to market, or for an evening out, but Walter did. All the time. It was the sort that Jennings used to wear in the fourth form of his minor public school in the 1950s: about an inch and a quarter wide, and had been washed and ironed so many times that it shone like a beacon. It bore some sort of motif: I was never sure whether this stood for some society or club of which Walter was a member.

I was standing in the kitchen of a timbered Herefordshire farmhouse. It was surrounded by some 250 acres of its own land but unfortunately, in estate agency terms, was ripe for modernisation. Walter probably thought so too but his decision to leave it as it was sprang from necessity rather than desire. The 400-yard track to the front door gave some indication of what was to come. It was more suited to a tractor ploughing competition. The garages around should have paid Walter commission for all the repair work that this little quarter-mile route produced. It was a journey I had made many times before, and somehow the potholes, like sand dunes in the desert, always seemed to appear in different places. Having bounced your way to the front of the house you were confronted by an enormous elm door. Oh, how I hated those doors. They never had a knocker and took every bit of skin off the knuckles as you struggled in vain to make the occupants hear you. This was always done under the watchful eye of the farm collie, sometimes assisted by a Jack Russell terrier. In fact, the eye wasn't so much watchful as intimidating. They always managed to give you a look that suggested a little nip to let you know who's boss wasn't totally out of the question.

Eventually, after hearing heavy feet tread the equally heavy stone floor, the huge piece of elm in front of me opened like a sideways-opening drawbridge. Walter was a man some twenty years my senior but, as was the tradition with many people in this part of the world, referred to me as 'sir'. At first I'd felt uncomfortable with this, but as time had gone by I'd grown used to it, and it had begun to seem as natural and reassuring as Hereford hops and Worcester china. As the door opened Walter welcomed me in with a warmth that was not matched by the temperature in the hall. It was a frosty day and Field House Farm was one of those houses where you ventured outside for a warm rather than stay inside. It had been in Walter's family for nearly 250 years and no doubt there had been some profitable times.

They were long gone. We were now in a time when economies of scale (among other reasons) rendered a farm of this size incapable of producing a living.

We were in the middle of probably the worst outbreak of foot and mouth disease known. Walter's small herd of cattle had gone, literally, up in smoke, for this was the way infected cattle were disposed of after they had been shot. Walter was at his wits' end. No money, no farm really without the stock, and no prospects. Farming was all Walter could do. For him, as for many of his sort, it was more than just a job: it was a way of life. The sad thing was that Walter's three sons were all out of the same mould. They were as honest and hard-working as the day was long but there was no money in running a farm like this for one man let alone four. The boys were as yet unmarried and likely to remain so – in financial terms and prospects they were definitely not the catch of the year.

Walter's wife, standing next to her stalwart husband, had the same, almost desperate air about her. She had tried the route of farmhouse bed and breakfast. While the hospitality had been second to none the general fabric of their home and the appalling first impression it gave ensured that few, if any, tourists knocked on that heavy old door. The threads on the carpet stood out like string and the curtains offered little if any protection from the light or eyes of those outside. Perhaps they should have marketed themselves as a time-warp weekend break.

I was stalling, trying desperately to think how I could break the news to Walter gently that his table was not about to end the run of bad luck the family had been having.

There in front of us was an oak dining table. It was very dark and heavily carved; it could almost have come from the Elizabethan or Jacobean periods. Farmhouse refectory tables that came from the late seventeenth and eighteenth centuries were now widely sought after, particularly by the wealthy city professionals who were moving out into the country and gutting and restoring homes like this one. The last good table I had sold had made something over £5,000. The pity of it was that we were not looking at a table like that. This one was of the type known to auctioneers as Jacobethan. They say the most important thing about a property is its location, and the second most important thing is location and the third most important thing is location. Well, with oak furniture you can simply swap the word location for colour. We were looking for a rich toffee colour. This one looked as if it had been dropped in a vat of treacle. People do not come knocking on your door to try to buy tables like this one. It was probably made in about 1900 and was worth a few hundred pounds.

And therein lay the problem. For Walter had always thought this was the real thing and the money would have been a lifesaver. It must have taken weeks of agonising to decide to sell the monstrosity, for that's what it was in truth, and now I had to tell him that his swan wasn't so much a goose as a muddy little duck.

He took it like a gentleman.

'I really hope I haven't wasted your time, sir, always thought it was the real thing. Still, these things are sent to try us.' The whisper was growing ever more hoarse.

As I watched his wife twisting her hands in her apron, trying and failing to conceal her chagrin, I think I almost felt worse than they did.

Then Walter continued, 'Before you go, sir, there is an old table in the potting shed which I don't suppose is worth anything but we could do with the space and if it won't sell it can go on the bonfire.' There was a pause as he remembered how his stock had been destroyed. 'Now I've got more time I can sort some of the odd jobs that need doing and the old shed's top of the list.'

I could well see why when we got to the end of the garden. The structure had been a shed – once. Now it was held up by the branch of a tree growing through the doorway; ivy was gluing the window in place and the corrugated iron on the roof was sieve-like in appearance and effect. Growing all around were stinging nettles of the most vicious breed. I tried to poke my head through the window. At first all I could see was a huge pile of old clay pots, but eventually I made out, emerging hesitantly from one side of the mass, something that looked like a gilt leg. It resembled the shape of a Jack Russell's front leg – the type that we called cabriole.

'Walter, it's a bit tricky even to see what it is.' But I felt I had to try to give him some hope to make up for the disappointment of the other table, so I added, 'Next time you're in Malvern with the trailer bring it into the sale-room and I'll have a look at it.'

And I thought nothing more about it. Life and work went on until about three weeks later when I was cataloguing in the saleroom and I heard the most extraordinary racket outside. Walter's Land-Rover resembled the track to his house: it was battered beyond belief and had probably missed the last one or five services. The holes in the exhaust meant that you couldn't fail to know Walter was around the corner, and for the hard of hearing there was the huge plume of blue smoke that erupted from the exhaust pipe at regular intervals. At the rear of the machine sat, rather incongruously, a sparkling stock trailer. Walter might go without: his stock most definitely didn't. He might travel second class but his animals had the best transport available. The irony now was there was no stock to occupy it.

The Land-Rover shuddered to a halt outside and Walter, complete with shining tie, jumped out. He walked apologetically round to the rear of the trailer. It seemed to take him an age to undo the back and let me see what he had brought. Walter would not dream of neglecting the formalities: the handshake and enquiries after health were essential parts of the greeting ritual, while I was itching to see the table. After what seemed an eternity he undid the bolts that held the back of the trailer in place. At last ... but then another delay ensued as Walter started to explain that he was really concerned about wasting my time. I quickly allayed his fears and he methodically began to lower the ramp. Then it appeared. A lovely, if rather worse for wear, eighteenth-century console table. A console table, or normally pairs of console tables, used to grace the grander mansion houses of the eighteenth century. They were designed to stand up against a wall, sometimes with a mirror above and often either side of the floor-to-ceiling windows that were so much a feature of the country houses of the landed gentry at that time. My glimpse through the ivy had not been enough to appreciate the jewel among all those pots. Hell, it looked a good thing, but like most of Walter's possessions it was a trifle battered. Once more he apologised for bringing it into the saleroom.

'If that proper table wasn't worth anything I don't hold out much hope for this,' he said. 'Reckon I should have used the diesel it's taken me to get here to start a decent fire with it.'

Walter was always concerned about wasting people's time, particularly those whom he regarded as professional men who wore suits to work. I hastily reassured him, being keen to start trying to find out more about the table as soon as I could. I knew it was eighteenth century and good, but I wanted to know how good. Walter looked anxious, which puzzled me a little. When I questioned him he eventually, and sheepishly, suggested that he would not have enough money to pay any fees for this work. I told him not to worry as it was part of my job and how I earned my fee. I told him that I'd let him know later when I'd done a bit of homework on it. And so off he went, clearly thinking I was quite mad.

It takes a lot to get me excited but this table succeeded. It was about three feet six inches wide, two feet six deep and three feet six high. The whole table was gilded and had carved decoration, like piles of old pennies formed as fish scales, cascading all down the legs, which was really unusual. It had a marble top plonked on it, but I was unsure whether this was original or not. It was all tatty, though, and there were chunks of white plaster showing through where the gilding had come off.

It was time to get the books out. I began to thumb through the relevant book on eighteenth-century English furniture. There were many books I could have looked at but this was the acknowledged bible. It contained all the important pieces from England's best houses that had been made by the major craftsmen of the period. I worked my way slowly and carefully through the section on tables: I didn't want to rush and miss my table. After about fifteen minutes I was coming to the end of the chapter – without success. Then I turned the page – and I couldn't believe it. There was my table. (All auctioneers feel when a piece comes into the saleroom, particularly a good piece, that it is their own personal possession until such time as it is sold.)

This was too good to be true. It was my table. The picture was only black and white, but none the less I could clearly see my table. Below each photo was a small caption giving the owner and location of each piece. 'HM The Queen, Hampton Court Palace', I read. I excitedly pored over the book's text, but found it annoyingly short of any useful information. It simply told the reader what a console table was and a little about the furniture at the palace, and stated that this table resided in Queen Charlotte's bedchamber. No mention of any maker, nor where it had originally been intended for; tables like this were normally made for a specific person or place.

It was now going-home time at the saleroom but this could not wait. I typed, as quickly as one finger allowed, a letter to the Queen's curator at Hampton Court, telling him that I was a provincial auctioneer with a table like the one illustrated in so-and-so's book and asking him for an opinion. It was an astonishingly slow process but I just made that evening's post, enclosing a rather grainy Polaroid photograph of the table with the letter.

Well, I thought, I'd better phone Walter and tell him what the score was with my table. He didn't seem overly concerned; perhaps he was still a little crestfallen that the Jacobethan monstrosity hadn't proved to be worth more, while the potting-shed table seemed to be stealing the limelight. His parting shot was, 'I'll leave it entirely up to you, sir.' That sort of responsibility made me worry all the more about doing the right thing by him.

The next day I waited by the phone,

almost expecting the Queen herself to call me to talk about my table. Nothing.

The following day I was at the office at nearly dawn, some two hours before the postman arrived, to open the letter that I was sure would arrive. Nothing.

This carried on for about a fortnight. Still nothing. I rang Walter to tell him as much and he almost seemed pleased that the Queen's curator obviously thought I was as mad as Walter did for getting excited about the potting-shed table. Walter's humour was based on a rich vein of experiences in life, not all of them favourable. The net result was a dryness just the far side of an un-buttered cheese cracker.

'Looks like the Queen won't be coming to bid for it herself then,' was quickly followed by, 'Pity we've only just let the bonfires go out. Still, it'll help start the next,' and, 'Knowing my luck I expect these tables have just been outlawed by a committee in Brussels.'

He was, though, nothing if not a gentle-man, and he went on to make it quite clear that, although he thought I was on a wild-goose chase, he appreciated the hope I was investing on his behalf. Walter was quite accustomed to setbacks in life. I was still optimistic: perhaps the man in the right department at the palace was on holiday? That would explain everything.

Then it happened. One Tuesday morning there was a letter in the post with the Hampton Court Palace crest on the back of it. I opened it, avid to absorb the contents, and it told me – nothing. Well, that's not strictly true: the curator did deign to agree that my photograph was similar to the table illustrated in old so-and-so's book, but that was all. It was a response but not quite the one I had been looking for. My vision of the Queen driving to Worcestershire, surrounded by attendants, all trying to buy my lovely table was evaporating very quickly.

I rang Walter and told him the news, or lack of it. I said that I wasn't going to let it lie there and that I would phone the man and have a chat with him. This elicited the usual response: 'I'll leave it entirely up to you, sir.'

I telephoned the Queen's curator, and told him that I was surprised that he wasn't overly excited about my table. Rather gently, he explained to me that, in his position, he was surrounded by wonderful things every day and it was quite easy to become blasé about them. While my table looked 'quite pleasing' I don't think he could understand what all the fuss was about. However, he was of course a gentleman too and he suggested that perhaps I should bring it up to London to show him and compare it to the one that was illustrated.

I telephoned Walter with these exciting new developments, which I have to say didn't seem to excite him very much, and back came the stock response.

On the day of the trip to the palace, Sophie, who worked with me, and I met at the saleroom early in the morning and loaded the base, but not the marble top which was just too heavy for the two of us to lift, into the Volvo estate.

As we drove we chatted about this extraordinary find. It obviously wasn't worth a fortune because of its condition and the top that might not be right, but it was still a delightful piece. It suddenly occurred to me that Walter had never once asked what the table was worth. It was almost as if he didn't want to be disappointed for a second time. Or maybe he felt I really had flipped and that it was best to humour me, until such time as I was whisked away to the auctioneers' rest home.

We got to the palace, which was exciting enough in itself, as the curator had provided a VIP parking space ticket. We had arranged to meet him at a certain time in the room with my table's twin. As we pulled the table out of the back of the car we looked at one another and both realised how much hope we were pinning on the four legs – very frail and battered ones – of an old table.

It was the height of the tourist season and

there seemed to be more Americans here than in New York. As we wandered around the palace looking for the right room we were the subjects of much attention and discussion among the tourists. Our progress reminded me of Charlie Drake and Tommy Cooper in the film *The Plank*, charged with the apparently simple task of carrying a plank of wood through town, which unwittingly led them into all sorts of trouble. Sophie and I were similarly helpless. I, thinking that my directions were spot-on, had backed the table and us both into what appeared to be a linen store. Reversing out of the store I was nearly run down by the stomach of a large American gentleman, which seemed to appear some time before the rest of him did. We apologised and moved as swiftly as two people carrying a table can along a corridor full of American tourists staring and pointing in our direction.

I had been appearing, albeit in a very minor role, in a television programme about antiques for BBC television. Clearly my celebrity status was stretching across the pond. I was just wondering how I could politely tell these Americans that, as we were running to a tight schedule, I probably wouldn't have time to stop and sign autographs. We struggled on as best we could, conscious that we needed to keep going. It was like hearing a police car or ambulance behind you and knowing that you have to either pull over or press on as fast as possible to clear the route. The problem was that the corridor was too narrow to pull over and it was difficult to go any faster with a table between us.

At least that was what I thought was happening. The reality was that our dear American cousins thought that we were pinching the table and trying to find a way out through the corridors of the palace. Sophie and I were in grave danger of being locked up on suspicion of theft from Her Majesty. I was beginning to panic when, in a flash of inspiration, I told them to look at the state of my topless shabby table: would the Queen have a piece like this in such poor repair? Then, as my senses at last prevailed, I told them the reason for our visit. This was finally backed up by the presence of the curator, who was looking for us and had heard the commotion. We rather sheepishly marched off to the room in question.

It was quite remarkable: on the left was my battered table showing signs of exposure to the Herefordshire elements; and on the right was this magnificent matching example. Matching in style anyway. The Queen's table was not of gilt wood but was made of a wonderfully patinated walnut. Patina is muck and grime (though I'm not sure how much of that the palace would have had) that furniture has picked up over a hundred years or more which is then polished, sometimes literally and sometimes simply by being handled, whereupon the natural grease in the hand does the job. Patina is the soul of a piece of furniture; it is the lines on its face and the wrinkles on its hands. It gives it character. The result in well-coloured walnut is a cross between chewed toffee and a rich honey colour. The Queen's table on the right had all of that and more.

The curator told me that records showed that the palace table was made for the then Prince of Wales in 1729 by a man called Benjamin Goodison. Goodison was a well-known cabinet-maker who had designed a lot of furniture for the prince. I asked him if this meant my table was also made for the prince. Apparently not definitely, for courtiers at that time had furniture made to imitate that of the royal family, but the style of the carving and decoration were definitely the handiwork of Goodison. Today I suppose we call that fashion. No curator will ever give an opinion of value but at least now I had found a relative for my piece and could, with some authority, say who made it. We then went on to talk about the top that I had left at Malvern. The curator said that it might have had a marble, or possibly wooden top, but that he couldn't say whether our top was original or not, particularly as we had left it

120 miles away back in the saleroom.

We drove home in good humour because we felt we had achieved something. When we got back to the sale-room in mid-afternoon it was time to call Walter again. I needed to discuss with him when and where he wanted to sell the table. No prizes for guessing Walter's reply. During the conversation, however, he seemed a bit quieter and more reserved than normal.

'Are you sure you're all right, Walter?' I asked. He was not a man to share his problems with the world so it took some coaxing before he revealed that the family's fortunes had taken a turn for the worse. He had no idea how, but a fire had broken out in the farm's implement store and destroyed the few antiquated mechanical relics that ran the farm. Ordinarily this would not have been a problem – the tractor and other tools were all very old and worth less than £4,000 and would have been covered by the insurance company – had Walter been able to afford to renew the last insurance policy. So no money to replace what had been destroyed, however ancient it had been. Walter, as usual, took it without a hint of complaint. His stock answer about leaving it all to me was meant to impress upon me how much confidence he had in me to make the most of the table – which was an added burden, but one I had to carry.

There were decisions to be made. I felt it was going to make over the £6,000 tax liability band and that this might affect when it should be sold. A realisation over £6,000 would result in the vendor having to pay capital gains tax. I also felt that with proper advertising the table would do well in my saleroom but also that I ought to offer Walter the reassurance of a London saleroom. I had a friend who worked for one of the major London salerooms and I asked him to come and have a look at the table, which he kindly agreed to do. After David, the London man, had done so, he spoke to a colleague and passed on the view that while it was good, it wasn't that special, and they gave me a figure that they felt it might make. It was make-your-mind-up time. There seemed little point in talking to Walter. He'd already told me, with regard to the tax angle, that he had more than enough losses to set any gain off against. As to where it should be sold, well, you already know what his reply to that would be.

I decided to trust my instincts and sell the table in my saleroom, having ensured that we notified as many potential buyers as we could and advertised it extensively. The weeks prior to the auction really were exciting as the sale adverts illustrating the table started to appear. People were interested in its history and how it came to be in

293

a Herefordshire farmhouse. This had also intrigued me. On more than one occasion I had asked Walter to rack his brain and turn out all the family papers to see if its history could be traced. This wasn't just idle interest on my part, as the full history or provenance from the day it had been made would have undoubtedly improved its value. All Walter could come up with was that the table had been in the family farmhouse since about 1900, which left a huge gap typical of the problems auctioneers face when dealing with such pieces. Unfortunately we were never to discover its early history.

Walter, who had watched the build-up of interest in his table with incredulity, was more convinced than ever that the whole antique world was stark raving mad. How could a scrubby potting-shed table be worth money, when a jolly good dining table like the one I was first asked to look at was relatively worthless? As it all seemed crazy to him, the question of the reserve price, below which the table would not be sold, was 'left entirely up to you, sir'. The responsibility weighed heavily on me. Suppose I had got it wrong and all these enquiries we had had were simply from people who were in on the conspiracy? No – I was sure we were going to be all right.

The sale day arrived.

There were some vendors whom auctioneers don't want at their sales – those whose emotions would get in the way. Sometimes their eagerness to sell is counterproductive. I was keen, however, for Walter to come. He didn't let me down. He, his wife and their three sons were all in attendance. Walter and his family had decided that they did not even want to know my views on what the reserve figure should be, leaving everything to me as they had done from day one. The whole saga had now become a source of amusement for them. They were completely at a loss as to how four legs could generate any excitement at all, without contemplating that a not insubstantial sum of money could be involved. As long as they did not have to take it back home all was well with the world. They were at last beginning to accept that it would sell rather than have to suffer the ignominy of the bonfire. This was a relief to them, primarily, I'm sure, as it would vindicate my reputation and not cause me to be taken off to the home for mad auction-eers. As Walter and his wife appeared, followed in line astern by their three hulking sons, I saw at once that each of the four men was now sporting one of Walter's famous shiny, dated ties. This was a new fashion for the sons and I hoped for their sake it did not catch on.

After the auction started I could see Walter's family sitting side by side, bolt upright, almost as if they were waiting in a doctor's surgery for some imminent bad news. Walter had been to more cattle market auctions than you could shake a stick at but the antiques world was a new arena for them all. They seemed terrified to move in case they bought something that they neither wanted nor could afford. As a result they all sat completely still, staring straight ahead, directly at me on the auctioneer's rostrum. This was not only unsettling but also somewhat hypnotic. I was beginning to feel like Mowgli in *The Jungle Book* being entranced by the snake when suddenly I got a slight prod in the ribs from Sophie who sat on my right on the rostrum. 'You okay?' she whispered. I started to gulp the water by my right hand, and pulled myself together.

The table was Lot 98. We had had a huge response during the time set aside for viewing the lots that were to be auctioned. Vendors often ask whether their goods would make more money if necessary repairs were carried out prior to sale. By and large the answer is no: buyers like to buy their goods market-fresh having spotted the potential, and then have the work done by their own restorers. It is a very personal thing. People, including the major English furniture dealers, had come from all over the country. We had also dealt with enquiries from throughout Europe and America. As we reached Lot 80 I began to get a little anxious, hoping that I had done as much as I could. Would it sell well? Were all the buyers there? I looked around, carefully avoiding Walter's family's eyes. I had some reassurance in that bidders who could not attend the sale in person had booked all our telephone lines to bid live during the auction. Surely that boded well? My table was not going to be my table for much longer.

'Lot 98, ladies and gentlemen, this lovely eighteenth-century console table attributed to Goodison, cabinetmaker to the Prince of Wales in 1729. Bid me. Where will you start?'

The bidding started at £8,000 and gradually crept up into the teens and then on to £20,000 and finally, going, going, gone and sold for £23,000. This was more than double the minimum suggested by the London auction house. I was absolutely delighted. At last I let myself look in the direction of Walter and his family. It was as if they had been turned to stone. They looked completely numb, and utterly white. After what seemed an eternity, a small smile appeared on Walter's face, which quickly spread to the rest of the family. It disappeared just as quickly when I moved on to the next lot. The stony stare was now back – the last thing they wanted was to buy something by accident, even if they could now afford it.

After the sale, as Walter and I chatted, he couldn't conceal his pleasure – not simply at the money that had suddenly been put in his pocket but that his faith in me had been repaid. Walter was perhaps too proud to say how this money was going to change their lives, but as his wife thanked me for the tenth time she gave my arm a squeeze of gratitude which meant more than any words. I was just so pleased that, by chance, I happened to pick up the right book just after Walter had dropped the table off and spotted that illustration.

I was overjoyed to know that financially the pressure was off this charming family. I secretly hoped Walter might buy himself a new tie, or perhaps something for his long-suffering wife. They had both come to view day to have one last look at the table. Just before they left she had come up to me and said, 'You know, Philip, I'm going to miss that table,' which surprised me, for sentimentality was something I had attributed to neither of them. But she went on, 'Many years ago we used to have it in the kitchen and that old marble top was the best thing in the world for making pastry on.'

Lot 20

Never Judge a Book by its Cover

I was standing in the main room of a rented sheltered accommodation apartment in Worcester. Sparse simply didn't go far enough to describe it; this was minimalism in the extreme. There was an old, dated sofa, a 1960s teak table with a black and white portable television on it and nothing else at all. The kitchen housed a fridge and a cooker of no value, while the bedroom had a worthless single bed and an Edwardian pine chest of drawers worth about £100. That was it.

I had been instructed by a firm of local solicitors to prepare a probate valuation in the estate of the late James Hedder who had died at the age of eighty-four.

Well, no matter how hard I looked I could see nothing else in the little flat and my valuation report had the words 'No commercial value' next to every item except the pine chest which I duly valued at £100.

I drove back to the office feeling quite sad for the late James Hedder. He had clearly lived an extremely frugal life for all his eighty-four years and now that he had died the sum total of his existence had been valued at £100. It just didn't seem right. He had obviously struggled through his years and had nothing to show for them.

I telephoned the solicitor acting in this matter to explain the brief nature of my report.

'Half expected it, Philip,' came the reply. 'Old James was a wizard on the stock market but hated the taxman. Vowed never to leave anything he could get his hands on. Must have been worth over half a million but gave it all away to avoid inheritance tax. He'd have been heartbroken to know that he'd left anything as valuable as that old chest.

'By the way, Philip, I've got a chair for you to look at. Apparently the client's cat sleeps on it but they think it might be quite good,' the lawyer continued. 'Pop in and have a look and tell me what you think.'

I did, but that's a lot for another sale.

The publishers hope that this book has given you enjoyable reading. Large Print Books are especially designed to be as easy to see and hold as possible. If you wish a complete list of our books please ask at your local library or write directly to:

Magna Large Print Books
Magna House, Long Preston,
Skipton, North Yorkshire.
BD23 4ND

This Large Print Book, for people
who cannot read normal print,
is published under the auspices of

THE ULVERSCROFT FOUNDATION

... we hope you have enjoyed this book.
Please think for a moment about those
who have worse eyesight than you ...
and are unable to even read or enjoy
Large Print without great difficulty.

You can help them by sending a
donation, large or small, to:

**The Ulverscroft Foundation,
1, The Green, Bradgate Road,
Anstey, Leicestershire, LE7 7FU,
England.**
or request a copy of our brochure for
more details.

The Foundation will use all donations
to assist those people who are visually
impaired and need special attention
with medical research, diagnosis
and treatment.

Thank you very much for your help.